W9-ASI-892

CLOSER TO
GOD

CLOSER TO
GOD

PETER LUNDELL

SPIRE

© 2009 by Peter Lundell

Published by Revell
a division of Baker Publishing Group
P.O. Box 6287, Grand Rapids, MI 49516-6287
www.revellbooks.com

Spire edition published 2012

Previously published under the title *Prayer Power*

ISBN 978-0-8007-8817-9

Printed in the United States of America

All rights reserved. No part of this publication may be reproduced, stored in a retrieval system, or transmitted in any form or by any means—for example, electronic, photocopy, recording—without the prior written permission of the publisher. The only exception is brief quotations in printed reviews.

Scripture is taken from the HOLY BIBLE, NEW INTERNATIONAL VERSION®. NIV®. Copyright © 1973, 1978, 1984 by Biblica, Inc.™ Used by permission of Zondervan. All rights reserved worldwide. www.zondervan.com

12   13   14   15   16   17   18   7   6   5   4   3   2   1

For Cec Murphey,
mentor
best friend
father of my writing

CONTENTS

Internal Helps

External Helps

Winning the Battles

Moving Out

ACKNOWLEDGMENTS

Kim, thank you for blasting open the possibilities of prayer in my life and for believing in me all these years. Cec, thank you for coaching me through transformation not just in how I write but in who I am. Mary Kay, thank you for excellent critiques, and thanks to the San Diego Christian Writers Guild cyber critique group. Gayle, thank you for your sharp observations and for helping me to find my voice and to be real to normal people. Vicki, thank you for taking a chance with my manuscript. And to all the staff at Baker Publishing Group, thanks for doing a great job.

FIRST WORD

Sometimes my son's brain seems to be in outer space." The dad bit his lip and stared across the empty park. "I can't get through to him."

I nodded my understanding, and the words slipped out as if by themselves: "The less I tried to fix my daughter and the more I prayed for her, the better she got. My wife had cancer, but she prayed like a madwoman and got healed."

"That's cool for you." He sighed and shook his head. "But I don't know the right words. And when I do pray, God seems beyond my reach."

He had read books on prayer and tried several times to pray regularly. But each time he floundered like a fish on the bottom of a boat, until he prayed only at mealtimes and at church. He wasn't happy about it, but he didn't expect much change for his son or for himself.

His world, my world, your world churns with needs. Sometimes they overwhelm. Do you ever feel as if your prayers hit the ceiling and bounce back down? Maybe you settle for praying enough to meet a minimum quota—whatever that is. And if you're "religious" enough, you may feel a tinge of guilt that you don't pray enough or the right way.

Let's forget about "have to," "ought to," and "should." I think most of us would love to connect more with God in the conversation of faith we call prayer. Yet most of us cannot (or would not) hide away in a monastery to learn how to pray better. That's okay, because God doesn't hang out only in monasteries. He lives and links up with us in the middle of our busy lives.

This book can help improve your connection with the one who created you and loves you. We'll look at people who have gone before us, what the Bible says, and practical ways to grow closer to God in prayer. Each day speaks to an essential facet of a dynamic prayer life and ends with a prayer starter for that particular area of prayer. An appendix at the end of the book has "growth gauges" and suggested activities corresponding to each day that can help you get an idea of where you are in each of the topics and what you could do to improve.

As you read this book, you may identify with the guy in the park. Like me, he's come to see that improving his connection with God is not a pipe dream—it's a reality within our reach. It takes time and commitment. It takes new habits. And it's worth it, even if the road is bumpy. Every day is God's gift of a new beginning.

Praying people usually find that the rewards surpass their expectations. Mother Teresa said, "Prayer enlarges the heart until it is capable of containing God's gift of Himself."[1] How big can our hearts grow?

Let's find out.

A HEART
AFTER GOD

— DAY 1 —

HUNGER FOR GOD

I said yes to pastoring a church that in twenty years had gone through fifteen pastors. And of those twenty years, the last two were without a pastor at all. Just about every bad thing that could happen in a church had happened there. But I was going to turn it all around.

I had committed to staying for at least five years. After four and a half years, I seriously evaluated myself and the church. We had some successes and had become a nice, evangelical congregation with lots of activities—but I felt as if we were on a treadmill. Though a few of the members were loyal and committed, others resisted change, such as my expectation to commit time and allegiance to God and to ministry.

No matter what we did, it seemed that our meetings, outreaches, and even picnics were uninspiring and repetitious. No one was happy—not me, not the church members, not even visitors.

I didn't seem able to lead them. At least, they weren't following.

I grew discouraged. I concluded that the only reason I attended the church was because I was the pastor.

I persuaded the members to agree to make changes—like pray more, follow my leadership and the Holy Spirit's leading, and step up to do more ministry. But most people found those changes too unfamiliar or too demanding. Some families moved away. Most left for other churches. More than 90 percent of the congregation walked out the door.

I felt like a worn-out rag.

I wrestled with the temptation to quit, but I sensed God had called me to stay with the church. So I decided to stay no matter what. I didn't know where else to go anyway. But my determination staggered under the burden of discouragement. I needed hope.

I could see that my academic degrees and ministry experience would not get me through this. And God didn't show any sign of giving me an easy way out. I took an inventory of my heart. I admitted I was tired of hearing what I ought to do. Tired of feeling that I was never good enough. Tired of letting church be a substitute for God.

I knew my biggest problem was with me and God, and I doubted he was the problem. I began to pray as I never had before: "Lord, take me past failure and success, past performance and being good. I want you. I want your Spirit to breathe in me.

Catch me up in something greater than my own life. I'm hungry for you, and I don't care what other people think. Everything else in my life fades compared to you."

The more I prayed, the more I wanted only God and what he intended for the church. My hope increased. My hunger for God increased. And to my surprise, new people came into the church.

Those who left lamented that the church didn't function the way it used to. One said it was going to hell. But the new people sensed the hope I had found. They too began to hunger for God. That hunger moved us toward a whole new experience of God—and a whole new church.

GETTING HUNGRY

Hunger for God is that deep desire to know and experience more of God. The prophet Isaiah felt it when he cried out, "My soul yearns for you in the night; in the morning my spirit longs for you" (Isa. 26:9).

Hunger for God often starts when the doctor says "cancer," when a husband dies, or when the boss delivers a termination notice. Times when no one can help but God.

Hunger for God often emerges when our daily grind leaves us weary, when life plateaus and unfulfilled dreams slip through the holes of an empty heart. We finally say, "God, I don't like change, but staying the same is worse. I'm hungry for you. Give me all of you. Do what you want to do in my life."

My hunger grew out of the tired desperation of life on a winding-down treadmill. A friend of mine endured a divorce and realized he'd never get out of this world alive, so he'd better wake up. We all have our own stories, our own struggles and blessings. Whoever we are, we can say, "Lord, I want more of you!" From that follows everything else in our prayer lives.

HUNGER GETS INTENSE

Hunger for God is a lot like hunger for food: we can wish for a snack or starve for a feast. I found that the hungrier I was, the more of God's presence I felt. It was up to me how close I felt to God and how much his presence lifted my attitude. I came to agree with A. W. Tozer, who says that God "waits to be wanted."[1]

Despite riches and power, King David had a huge hunger for God: "O God, you are my God, earnestly I seek you; my soul thirsts for you, my body longs for you, in a dry and weary land where there is no water" (Ps. 63:1). Can you feel that verse? "Earnestly," "thirsts," "longs." David's hunger for God is so strong that he feels it in his physical body. Then he says, "Because your love is better than life, my lips will glorify you" (v. 3).

Do you ever crave that "better than life" experience of God's love? The sons of Korah did: "My soul yearns, even faints, for the courts of the Lord; my heart and my flesh cry out for the living God" (Ps. 84:2). These guys are so hungry for God, they're ready to faint! They're emotional, even physical about it.

Psalm 143:6 gives us a concrete picture of hunger for God: "I spread out my hands to you; my soul thirsts for you like a parched land." This is ground where the grass is dead, ground so dry it cracks.

I know how that ground feels. I need the Holy Spirit's abundance in my life. Just *wanting* that abundance has changed my prayer life. Hunger drives me—drives us—to seek God more. And he waits for us to want him.

DETERMINE TO BE HUNGRY

Despite all that, sometimes I don't feel like praying. I've got lots of reasons: I'm too busy, I'm tired, I prayed enough yesterday. That's when I say, "Lord, increase my hunger for you. I want more of you!"

People have hungered for God all through history, besides in the Bible. John of the Cross, a sixteenth-century Spanish monk, was just a little guy—but he had an enormous hunger for God. He tried to show what that hunger was like by drawing a diagram that depicted the top of Mount Carmel as spiritual union with God. All sorts of other desires lined up on either side, but a single-minded, passionate focus on God pierced straight through to the top. John ultimately desired God himself, not his gifts or blessings. Instead of seeking the rewards the world offered, or even the rewards God offered, he emptied himself of desires and gave himself to God. On top of the diagram, he wrote of those very rewards, "I have them all without desire."[2] John experienced the truth of what Jesus taught: "Seek first [God's] kingdom and his righteousness, and all these things will be given to you as well" (Matt. 6:33). When we put God first, everything else follows.

Hunger for God is the heart of prayer. Without hunger for God, nothing can improve our prayer lives. The truth is, unless we're hungry, we probably won't pray much. When we want God more than anything else, we'll continually talk with him.

We Leak!

Hunger for God is a continual craving. Just as eating a big dinner still leaves us hungry the next day, a meaningful experience of God eventually gives way to spiritual dryness. We can also think of our spiritual lives as a bucket. God's Spirit fills us the way water fills a bucket. Sin, stress, and the busyness of life poke holes in the bucket. Giving our time and energy to care for others, and apparently just being human, poke holes. And we leak. Developing a hungry—or thirsty—mind-set keeps us getting refilled. When we recognize that all the things that claim to satisfy won't, habitual desire for God becomes more and more natural.

I was looking for something that would keep me hungry and wanting to be refilled.

A Sense of Eternity

Feeling God's nearness was great. Yet I was looking for a whole new way of thinking that would keep me pointed toward God, despite how I felt or whether my prayers got answered. I found what I was looking for spread all over the Bible: a sense of eternity. A sense of eternity means I realize how short my life is, and how everything I do on earth can be done with an awareness of heaven. It helps me remember what's truly important. The results can be eternal. Here are a few verses that express that:

- Psalm 39:4—"Show me, O LORD, my life's end and the number of my days; let me know how fleeting is my life."
- Psalm 90:12—"Teach us to number our days aright, that we may gain a heart of wisdom."
- Psalm 103:15–17—"As for man, his days are like grass, he flourishes like a flower in the field; the wind blows over it and it is gone, and its place remembers it no more. But from everlasting to everlasting the LORD's love is with those who fear him."
- Ecclesiastes 7:2—"It is better to go to a house of mourning than to a house of feasting, for death is the destiny of every man; the living should take this to heart."
- James 4:14—"Why, you do not even know what will happen tomorrow. What is your life? You are a mist that appears for a little while and then vanishes."

If we internalize the message of these verses, nothing—absolutely nothing—in this world will hold the importance to us that it did before. A sense of eternity frees us from the burden of demands and desires in this world. Freedom *from* the world is freedom *for* God.

The Best Thing in Life

I have come to believe that the best thing we can have in life is not family, not love, not even receiving Jesus. The best thing in life is a hunger for God, because we will always get more of him. This hunger leads nonbelievers to faith in Jesus and believers to greater experiences of Jesus. Hunger for God always leads us closer to him. Whether in this life or eternity, what could be better?

PRAYER
~ Starter ~

Lord, put in my heart a continual hunger for you. Above all the things you give me, I want more of you. . . .

—— *DAY 2* ——

INTIMACY WITH GOD

A weathered gravestone along a dirt road in upstate New York stands as the only reminder of one of the greatest men of prayer who ever lived. We have no surviving photographs of him, no letters or notes. He wrote no books or articles. Few have written about him. We have no idea what he did before he was forty, when he took his first pastorate, or if he had any descendants. His name was Daniel Nash—the sacrificial powerhouse of prayer behind the nineteenth-century evangelist Charles Finney and some of the greatest spiritual revivals ever to burst on a populace.

With Finney in the limelight, Nash went mostly unnoticed. Whether praying alone or with others, he sought no public recognition. He concerned himself with one audience: God. This was a guy who cultivated deep intimacy with God and showed no interest in whether anyone else even knew him.

Nash's hunger for God led him into an intense and intimate prayer life. He traveled ahead of Finney to towns where they had scheduled meetings. He secluded himself in rented rooms, even basements, where he prayed for days and sometimes weeks. He often groaned and agonized, exhausting himself as he prayed. His countless hours in God's presence seem to have played a major role in the conversions of thousands. Finney and Nash led the only revival ministry ever known to retain 80 percent of converts.[1]

I'm not Daniel Nash, but his example has taught me to spend time alone with God. I have seen how intimacy with God can positively influence everything in my life. Intimacy is worth spending any amount of time necessary. When I get caught up in busyness and relegate my leftover time to God, an empty feeling rises in me, and I crave time with God until I satisfy it.

INTIMACY WITH GOD

Hebrews 4:15 tells us that Jesus is our high priest, "who has been tempted in every way, just as we are—yet was without sin." He knows what we go through. God encourages us to "approach the throne of grace with confidence" (v. 16). We don't have to wallow at a distance, feeling guilty because we blew it. He invites us to approach him at his very throne, where he offers us "mercy and . . . grace to help us in our time of need" (v. 16). Imagine it: a personal audience with the Creator of the universe.

The Creator calls himself "Daddy." That's the literal translation of *Abba*, the word the New Testament uses. Intimacy with our heavenly dad has nothing to do with a method. It's a relationship. It's acting on our privilege of being his children—being close to him simply because we're his. It's concentrating on God himself, not on what he gives us. His Spirit lives inside us. The Bible says our physical bodies are his temples (1 Cor. 3:16–17; 6:19). We can't get more intimate than that.

Most people experience this nearness to God in a setting where they are uninterrupted. The feeling might be of peace, joy, conviction of sin, intensity of purpose, or even ecstasy. The setting might be a church sanctuary or a secluded room, or perhaps a mountain, a beach, or a garden. Once in a while the experience may come like a flash in a busy marketplace. I have encountered this normally gentle (but occasionally overwhelming) sense of God's nearness in all of these places. Maybe you have too. The feeling is sometimes "ahh," sometimes "wow!"

Teresa of Avila, mentor to John of the Cross, was a sixteenth-century Spanish party-girl-turned-nun who led a reform movement among nuns and established fourteen convents. She struggled through long, dry periods of prayer to break into deep intimacy with God, complete with supernatural visions. In her book *Interior Castle*, she describes a believer's life as a castle made of crystal. God stands at the center and shines out, but the shining light is darkened by sin and anything that separates us from God. Our spiritual journey leads us inward through the castle and its stages of spiritual growth, moving us ever closer to God until we and God are like two wax candles with one flame.[2] She insists that such intimacy is available to those of us who persistently seek God. Imagining God's point of view, she says, "The soul of the just person is nothing else but a paradise where the Lord says he finds his delight."[3]

Similarly, King David prayed, "One thing I ask of the LORD, this is what I seek: that I may dwell in the house of the LORD all the days of my life, to gaze upon the beauty of the LORD and to seek him in his temple" (Ps. 27:4). "One thing," David said. Jesus echoed this when he said to Mary and Martha, "Just one thing is needed. Mary has chosen what is better, and it will not be taken away from her" (Luke 10:42). One thing.

David wanted one thing. Martha lacked one thing. Mary chose one thing. Me? Too often I chase many things. So I'm taking lessons from guys like Moses, who focused only on God when he climbed Mount Sinai and when he sat in the tent of meeting. Most leaders in the Bible understood this singular focus. Intimate God encounters changed their prayers, their lives, and their legacies. They'll change ours too.

LIFE GIVING

Intimacy with God may be the most life-giving experience on earth. Physically, our lives derive from God's miracle of reproduction through our parents. Spiritually, our spirits are given life when we are "born again," or "born from above" (John 3:3). The more we connect with God, our source of both physical and spiritual life, the more we experience the love, joy, hope, forgiveness, and grace that comes from him. When I became a believer, God didn't save me only from going to hell. He saved me from myself. Growing close to God showed me that his abundant life far surpassed anything else I chased after.

When I trim vines in my backyard, the leaves wither within hours. No connection, no life. We're the same. When we stay connected with God, we are spiritually vital. We may neglect our attachment to God and feel fine for a while. But invariably we'll wither inside, like a leaf cut from the vine. Jesus describes a vine and its branches in John 15:4, saying that if we abide, or remain, in him, like the vine we will be fruitful.

Psalm 84:10 expresses the feeling of joy in God's presence: "Better is one day in your courts than a thousand elsewhere." For the people of the Old Testament, being in the courts of the Lord meant hanging around the tabernacle and later the temple, and was Old Testament–speak for "We're in God's presence." If we add up the days, we find that one day in God's presence was worth more to them than three years anywhere else. Whether or not we read the verse literally, we see how precious it was to them to be connected with God. Along with them we can say, "Lord, I love to spend time in your presence."

IT WILL COST US

This intimacy comes at a price. Dietrich Bonhoeffer writes, "When Christ calls a man, he bids him come and die."[4] Dying here is dying to oneself, which means turning away from desires and habits that would keep us from Christ. Paul expresses this in Galatians 2:20: "I have been crucified with Christ and I no longer live, but Christ lives in me. The life I live in the body, I live by faith in the Son of God, who loved me and gave himself for me." Dying to ourselves is hard and needs clean, or at least repentant, hearts.

Most of us struggle here. I have. But our struggles become our opportunities to cling to God's grace—his endless love and mercy that we don't deserve. Philippians 2:13 describes this part of grace in action: God "works in [us] to will and to act according to his good purpose." God's grace moves us into spiritual maturity.

We may say, "Yes! I will die to myself and grow more intimate with God." But a lot of us own way-too-busy schedules. In the story of Martha and Mary (Luke 10:38–42), Martha had a full to-do list. Mary had her list too. We all have them. But Mary chose to put Jesus at the top of her list and let everything else get done later. The same choice is ours. Though we sometimes falter, the habit of putting time with God first will become more and more natural as we make that deliberate, daily decision.

Intimacy with God will cost us—through spending time, changing priorities, and turning away from sin. But lack of intimacy will cost us even more—we may have higher levels of stress, depression, anger, disorientation, exhaustion. . . . We can easily see how intimacy with God is its own reward.

LET GO TO RECEIVE

Though intimacy costs us, we need to be careful of striving for it. Perhaps you've *tried* to go to sleep, or *tried* to make someone love you, or *tried* to be worthy of God's approval. All three have one thing in common: futility.

Intimacy is the same. We don't find it by striving but by receiving. If intimacy in prayer were a physical place, it would be a secluded garden. Though secluded gardens need tending (which is work), they are primarily places to rest, enjoy, and feel restored. We tend to meet God in these places, as if we reserve a garden bench for us and God to simply spend time together—with no intrusions allowed.

King David says, "My soul finds rest in God alone" (Ps. 62:1). That verse can also be translated, "My soul waits in silence for God alone." Intimacy comes when we stop striving after God and instead quiet down . . . open up . . . and receive.

PRAYER
~ *Starter* ~

Lord, draw me into deep, personal intimacy with you. I want to spend time with you, draw closer to you, and experience you more. . . .

— DAY 3 —

HOLY PASSION

When I studied in the Fuller Seminary library in Pasadena, California, I was intrigued by a woman who smiled at everyone. Once or twice every hour someone would pull her away from her studying. Ten, twenty, or thirty minutes later she would return alone. I asked myself, *Who is this?*

One evening in the cafeteria line she took my tray by mistake, so I sat down with her.

Her name was Kim. She immediately leaned forward and asked, "Have you been filled with the Holy Spirit? Will you go to a 6:00 a.m. prayer meeting tomorrow?"

No, I wasn't filled, and no, I wouldn't pray at 6:00 a.m. I didn't get up that early for anyone. I didn't think God was awake at that hour. But that evening something kept telling me to go.

The next morning at 6:00, I began to discover the meaning of holy passion. Kim, along with a dozen other "early Christians" as they called themselves, was passionate about people knowing Jesus and connecting with him. I had been wondering how much of the Bible was really true, and here she was praying Bible promises into reality. I was asking intellectual questions about God, and she was satisfying those questions not with academic answers but with a burning heart.

Kim and I are now in our third decade of marriage, and people still pull her away for the same reasons they did at the library. They see her passion for what God will do in people's lives. The love of God is so big in her heart that she cares, teaches, and prays for people until she drops. I've had to catch her on her way down. I've also caught some of her passion.

OVERCOMING COMPLACENCY AND DISTRACTIONS

Fervency can fall asleep under a blanket of complacency—the calm, secure sense of satisfaction with our lot in life, the feeling that everything is okay (or at least tolerable) and we've little need to strive for anything. Complacency is perilous to believers. It waylays us from pursuing God's call. It keeps us from caring about a lost world. It blinds us from seeing the devil's deceptions. Complacency is subtle, respectable, and justifiable. But it lulls us into spiritual sleep. Anyone who lives a comfortable life, or gets exhausted from a difficult life, is subject to complacency. I've found that hunger for God overcomes complacency because it sparks and fuels passion.

Has your desire to pray ever gotten tangled or distracted? If it's not endless demands on your time that distract you, it might be a messy house, kids (or parents), grass to cut, TV, computer games, or the mall. I've finally gotten to a stage in life where I'm not distracted by everything in sight. And I no longer get disillusioned (and therefore complacent) because I fail to do everything that others think I should. My midlife crisis taught me to focus on being who God created me to be and doing what he created me to do. I no longer care about anything else. I can hardly express how liberating that is. Similarly, holy passion burns with singular focus—a flame that, when it has enough fuel and energy, can turn into a blowtorch.

In the story of Jesus' overturning the money changers' tables (John 2:13–17), Jesus' disciples stare in amazement at his bold audacity. Then they remember Psalm 69:9: "Zeal for your house consumes me." Throughout Scripture, the temple—the house of God—represents God's presence. Jesus was consumed with passion for God. Psalm 104:4 says that the Lord makes "flames of fire his servants." Having a holy passion means we grow zealous about what the Lord has called us to do. We can genuinely pray, "Burn in me, O Spirit of God—and make me your fuel!"

PASSION AND THE OBJECT OF PRAYER

Passion usually works its way into action. Whatever our personality, getting involved in God's calling usually breeds passion. And passion in turn fuels our involvement in what we do. It may be volunteering in a local church or social welfare organization.

It could extend to disaster relief or overseas missions. It could be full-time or part-time, giving or going. In causes that involve life and death, the passion can be all-consuming.

Anyone can do this in big or little ways. From my first days as a believer, I had a passion for world missions. So I went to India for several months and worked with Samjee Kallimel, an apostle to lepers and the poorest of the poor. My passion eventually spread to my whole church, who started praying and sacrificially donating to him. Now church members themselves want to go help him, and so the cycle continues. I'm sure if you think about it, you could find an example or possibility in your own life.

To keep that passion from choking or stagnating, I find it helps to simplify our lives and to exit the comfort zones.

A SIMPLIFIED LIFESTYLE

Could it be that our loaded-with-possessions, squeeze-in-every-activity, choked-in-credit-card-debt lives are too complicated? Yep. Complications infiltrate our lifestyle like weeds. Richard Foster uses the terms *muchness* and *manyness*.[1] When our lives get crowded and pressured by things to do, take care of, or pay for, we have a problem with muchness and manyness. Some of us fill our lives with activities and possessions in order to gain a sense of fulfillment. Others get caught up in a world addicted to muchness and manyness. Sadly, pressuring ourselves or others this way leaves us feeling empty and distant from God. Jesus repeatedly warned us about the seductive power of possessions. In the parable of the sower, he said it's like thorns that choke the seed (Matt. 13:22). In the parable of the rich fool, he describes how it leads to a person building bigger storage facilities to hoard earthly wealth—then dying (Luke 12:16–21). Jesus also said in Luke 6:20, "Blessed are you who are poor." In part he was saying that the poor rarely have a problem with muchness and manyness. Possessions don't get between them and God.

Jesus extended hope to everyone when he said in Matthew 5:3, "Blessed are the poor in spirit"—those who have the meekness and simplicity of a poor person. To improve our prayers, most of us should consider simplifying our lives—by reducing piled-up possessions, overcrowded schedules, and financial obligations wherever we can. Some things we can't reduce. But when we can cut down our clutter, it increases our feeling of freedom. It also frees us to focus on more important things. The simpler our lives become, the better we connect with God.

EXIT THE COMFORT ZONES

Our prayers reflect what we think of God. J. B. Phillips believed that most people have a distinctly small concept of God. They don't expect much out of him, so they don't receive much from him. In his classic *Your God Is Too Small*, he writes, "The trouble with many people today [in 1952] is that they have not found a God big enough for modern needs. While their . . . horizons have been expanded to the point of bewilderment by world events and by scientific discoveries, their ideas of God have remained largely static."[2]

Isn't that what happens when we store our ideas of God in a religious box—neat and ready for use each Sunday morning? It also happens when we stay within our comfort zones. Each of us probably has more comfort zones than we realize. We're used to praying for small things that might be answered through time, medicine, or human effort.

But what happens when we deliberately try things that we normally would not—things that stretch us and that we cannot do on our own? We have to depend on God—just as we do when we're in trouble. At times I've tried things I normally wouldn't, then wanted to run like a scared guinea pig back into my cage. But that's what comfort zones can become: cozy cages that keep us from becoming what we could. Few things light prayer on fire like desperately throwing ourselves on God's mercy.

In my twenties I spent seven months working with a mission in Haiti. Some of my comfort zones stretched. The rest broke. Every time we went anywhere, we weren't sure if the roads would be passable, or if our truck would break down, or how we would get out if we got stuck in a river crossing. Sickness could hit any of us at any time. Our financial support from home sometimes didn't come through. Roofs on building projects collapsed. Supplies were unavailable. Scary-looking guys with guns stopped us at checkpoints on the road. Voodoo and demons ran rampant. I prayed a lot. I prayed with passion—I had to. And it was good for me.

When a crisis forces us out of a comfort zone, we still have the choice of how to respond. If we see the crisis as an indirect opportunity to grow, the problem will become a painful blessing waiting to happen. Not easy, I know. But which is easier to live with: seeing only a problem, or finding something positive within it? Pursuing the opportunity hidden in a problem is ultimately the easier—and more prosperous—way to deal with it.

Challenges and problems can be best friends to fervent prayer, as well as to our whole lives.

PRAYER
~ *Starter* ~

O God, burn in my heart the things that burn in
yours. Lead me into passionate pursuit of your
plan for my life today and in the future. . . .

— *DAY 4* —

STARTING A DEAD ENGINE

When the automobile was first invented, no one had conceived of a starter. So while one person sat at the wheel, another person stood in front of the car and cranked a handle connected to the engine. Round and round they'd heave the crank until the engine started running on its own. This led to phrases like "crank the engine" and "crank it up."

Sometimes prayer may feel like a dead engine, and it takes deliberate cranking to get the communication started and running on its own.

Too many times I have experienced the truth of Jesus' words: "The spirit is willing, but the body is weak" (Mark 14:38). I may sit or stand or walk while I try to talk with God, but my mind is like a dead engine. If I pray later in the day, I will usually be distracted—like a disconnected engine. These are points where, as is often said, I "start in the flesh and end in the Spirit."

Starting in the flesh and ending in the Spirit means that we may not feel like praying, but we pray anyway, using whatever help we can get. As we do this, our prayer starts to flow naturally.

PRAYER-PROMPTING PROBLEMS

Do you notice that every time a major tragedy occurs, the people involved, the whole general public, and even the media warm to the idea of prayer? Plenty of folks who have trouble remembering God even on Sunday will morph into passionate believers when facing a meltdown at the company or a spouse walking out the door. Problems can be very motivational, especially for seeking God. So they're not entirely bad. And all God's children have them.

When we recognize problems as opportunities to tap into what God can do, we'll always have incentive to start our prayer engine. Even if the only thing we can see is the problem, if it pushes us to pray, it's a step in the right direction. And if our own lives are nearly perfect, all we need to do is care about other people. They've got plenty of their own problems to stimulate our prayers.

WRITTEN PRAYERS

A second way to crank up prayer is by using written prayers. Some Christians may dismiss written prayers as leftovers of a formal church style they'd just as soon bury. If we use written prayers to mouth our way through rituals or as a substitute for our own prayers, then yes, bury them. Yet when we feel down or dull, reading a prayer may get us going when otherwise we wouldn't pray at all. When we read the prayer and truly pray it as we read, the written prayer becomes our own expression to God.

Reading written prayers can stimulate our own prayers when we internalize the words and express them as if they were our own. This gets the flow of our thoughts going. Then we can set the written prayer aside and go on praying.

Here are some examples of written prayers.

THE LORD'S PRAYER

The Bible gives us two versions of the Lord's Prayer to choose from: Matthew 6:9–13 and Luke 11:2–4. Meditating or praying about things related to each line, slowly and one at a time, can lead us into a wide spectrum of prayer. Here is a synthesis of Matthew's and Luke's versions, with those things we can meditate on in parentheses:

- Our Father in heaven (God as loving, intimate Father; present and eternal glories of heaven)
- Hallowed be your name (holiness of God and our living a life of holiness; character of God and promises of the many different names and references for God)
- Your kingdom come, your will be done (many manifestations of God's kingdom; seeking and following God's will)

- On earth as it is in heaven (God's work being done on earth here and now)
- Give us this day our daily bread (trusting God's daily provision for every need)
- Forgive us our sins as we also forgive those who sin against us (receiving God's forgiveness; forgiving others)
- Lead us not into temptation, but deliver us from the evil one (resisting temptation; deliverance and victory in spiritual battles)
- Yours is the kingdom and the power and the glory forever (God's glory and power revealed in our lives now and in his kingdom forever)

THE PRAYER OF ST. FRANCIS

This prayer, attributed to St. Francis of Assisi, has blessed people for hundreds of years. It can be found in different variations and goes essentially like this:

> Lord, make me an instrument of your peace,
> that where there is hatred, I may bring love;
> where there is wrong, I may bring forgiveness;
> where there is doubt, I may bring faith;
> where there is despair, I may bring hope;
> where there is sadness, I may bring joy;
> where there is darkness, I may bring light;
> O Divine Master, grant that I may seek to comfort
> rather than be comforted;
> to understand than to be understood;
> to love than to be loved;
> for it is in giving that we receive;

it is by forgiving that we are forgiven;
it is by dying that we are born to eternal life.[1]

MY PRAYER

Here is a prayer I wrote that encompasses many of the types of things I pray. Like most written prayers, it can be said as is, or each paragraph could be a prompt for additional spontaneous prayers.

I praise and worship you this day, Father, Son, and Holy Spirit. You are the Creator and Lord of the universe, and I thank you for creating and redeeming me. Lead me to be more like Jesus today, especially in [name an area for personal growth].

Form in me a pure heart that says no to sin and yes to loving you. I empty myself of selfish, sinful desires. Fill me with love and faith. Fill me with your Spirit, and lead me this entire day.

I trust you to meet all my needs according to the promises of your Word. So I put today's concerns into your hands: [name concerns].

Lead me into what *you* want me to do today. Lead me to love others the way you love me.

Protect my loved ones and me from the evil one.

Wherever I fall short, Lord, have mercy on me.

And to all these things I say, "Yes, Lord!" Amen.

PSALMS AND OTHERS

The largest source of written prayers is the book of Psalms, the prayers and songs of Israel. With 150 to choose from, we can always find one to start off our prayer. We have psalms of praise, comfort, and encouragement. Most of all we find laments—over a third of the Psalms begin with complaints. (People are often surprised to discover that God actually lets us complain to him.) These psalms start with expressing sadness or frustration to God. Then they generally progress toward finding hope. They're a great example of dumping our problems on God and turning to the path of faith and optimism.

Look for other prayer sources on the Internet, in books of collected prayers, or through subscriptions to monthly devotional guides.

PRAISE AND WORSHIP— LIVE OR RECORDED

A third way to crank prayer is through music. Many times I begin a prayer time by singing a song. Sometimes I will plunk on my guitar; sometimes I'll just sing. God doesn't seem to mind when I'm off-key. Playing an instrument or singing to God as the audience naturally moves the flow of worship into a flow of prayer. It is no accident that churches commonly precede prayer times with music, then continue to play it in the background as people pray. Music helps focus our attention and moves our emotions to connect with God.

Even if you don't play an instrument, or if you scare yourself when you sing, you can always listen to someone else worship—and join in. Any of us can turn on an electronic device and worship along with the music the way we would if we were with other people. At some point we'll tell the

Lord in our *own* words what the song is proclaiming or what we feel led to pray.

PRAYER NOTEBOOKS AND LISTS

A fourth way to crank our prayer is to use a prayer notebook or a list of prayer topics. Praying through a list may feel forced at first, but just as an airplane builds the necessary speed on its way down a runway for takeoff, lists give us clear substance, focus, and direction—the thrust we sometimes need for our prayer to take off. A notebook can be detailed or simple. Use what feels natural for you and stimulates your prayer. I'll talk more about this in day 19.

However we start the engine, it helps to focus the beginning of our prayer on God rather than on our endless needs. When we praise, honor, and thank God—and confess sin and receive forgiveness—we set our hearts right with him and keep our prayer focused not on our needs but on the one who meets them.

PRAYER
~ *Starter* ~

Expand on the Lord's Prayer: *God, you are truly my heavenly Father. You love me so much. Fill me with your presence and keep my eyes toward heaven. I love you, Lord. . . .*

— DAY 5 —

GETTING A FAITH LIFT

As I trudged to my seminary apartment one day, I mumbled and grumbled at God. Kim and I had clearly felt God leading me not to get a salaried job but rather to give myself to youth ministry and trust him to provide for our needs. Now the rent was past due, with no provision from God. I had prayed with faith, but got nothing. *Thanks a lot, God.*

As I stepped inside, Kim smiled and held up a check. Someone had sent us enough for the rent plus a week's worth of groceries. I went into the bedroom and dropped to my knees. "Lord, I was a fool. Forgive me for not trusting you."

The next month it happened again. We needed money, we didn't have money, I complained, God came through. Kim had faith and God responded. But I often found myself complaining.

Similar story lines played again and again, and each time I embarrassed myself by not trusting God and then being ashamed after he showed himself faithful. I am not kidding when I say this: the main reason I grew in faith was to avoid having to repent all the time.

With faltering steps I learned to trust God. Through each episode I felt as if he dangled me a little farther over a cliff and asked, "Will you trust me now?" Believing God for answered prayer takes us beyond—sometimes way beyond—rational thinking. Some might call this naive or misguided, but the point where we let go of our own abilities is where God responds.

LIFTING FAITH

I often see that God builds our faith and grows us as people by guiding us through hard times—the way a kite rises against the wind. Without wind resistance a kite will not climb, just as our personal growth will be limited if we have no problems. Even with wind, if a kite isn't grounded by a string, it will never get off the ground. And even if it did, it would flounder and fall. That string is like our prayer connection to God, who holds us in the buffeting winds of adversity. Cut the string or let it go, and the kite will fall. Hold the string tight, and the kite will rise. When we're tied to God, we will rise—and our faith will grow—in the face of hardship.

Some hardships rise from challenges we choose. My jaw dropped when I first learned about George Müller. His faith and God's calling stretched him beyond what most of us would dare (I'm still trying to figure this guy out), but his life of faith has encouraged thousands. After Müller emigrated from Germany to England in the mid-nineteenth century, he felt that God was leading him to build an orphanage for a hundred children. He built it—without any appeals for funds and solely on God's sovereign moving of people's hearts in response to his prayers. He continually depended on God to feed the orphans: "Often money had to be prayed in before breakfast could be eaten or the evening meal finished."[1] Many gifts arrived "at the very *instant of prayer*."[2]

One day a woman received an envelope from her daughter intended for Müller's orphanage. It sat there for several days before the woman brought it to Müller, who was in dire need. He wrote, "That the money had been so near for several days without being given is plain proof that it was in the heart of God to help us; but because he delights in the prayers of his children, he had allowed us to pray so long . . . to try our faith and to make the answer so much the sweeter."[3]

I find it instructive to our debt-saturated society that Müller never went into debt and never bought or built anything on credit. He always paid cash. He carefully kept his purchases in line with what he believed would honor God. In so doing, he felt he could trust God for every need. And God honored him in return by meeting his needs.

Müller continually received more children, built more buildings, and started more ministries. Eventually he housed, fed, and educated two thousand orphans.

Like anyone else who has grown in faith, Müller started small. As he trusted God for little things, he grew to trust God for big things. Through all his difficulties, he never shrank back. Though Müller lived in a league all his own, we can all follow his example and start with small things until we grow to trust God for big things.

ACCORDING TO OUR FAITH

In Matthew 9, a woman who had endured a hemorrhage for twelve years reached out and touched Jesus. He said to her, "Your faith has healed you" (v. 22). When two blind men followed Jesus, asking for mercy, he asked if they believed he was able to heal them. "Yes, Lord," they replied. Jesus said, "According to your faith will it be done to you" (v. 29). And they were healed.

Whenever Jesus worked miracles or changed people's lives, it was according to their faith. If you're like me, you may have found that if you do not believe God will act, he will work according to your low faith and not act. But if you believe he will, he'll probably do something awesome.

Have your experiences of God fallen short of the marvels you read about in Scripture? Mine have—but let's remember that most of those folks lived ordinary lives most of the time. And beware of this: when we don't experience miraculous power, our expectations easily sink to the level of our experiences. We can change that result by committing to trust God no matter what we experience—even if we feel foolish about it. Our experiences will tend to rise to the level of our faith. Jesus is unambiguous: he responds to our needs according to our faith. Many times I have clenched my teeth and said, "Lord, despite my experiences, I choose to trust what you promise in your Word. Even if I don't see your answer soon, I will keep trusting." Be it healing, financial provision, or guidance, my experiences have usually risen to the level of my faith.

I've found that God knows better than we do how to answer us. I prayed for a good job and was offered a well-paying position packed with fringe benefits. But God led me to take the youth ministry job that had no benefits and didn't pay enough—the one I grumbled about earlier. A year later I added up the many gifts and special offerings given me in thanks for what God had done in the kids' lives. I sat back, eyes wide—I was better off financially than I would have been had I taken the well-paying job. Plus I reaped the blessings of priceless experiences I would not have had otherwise.

How many times have you had to wait for God's answer to your prayer? Sometimes we wait for his divine timing, or he waits for us to get over our stubbornness. Other times God delays his answer so we will grow in faith and persistence. When we realize that his purposes are greater than the things we ask for, we begin to understand how he works and why. Then we can see the wisdom of hanging on despite the circumstances.

When we're tired, distracted, or discouraged, faith can be as basic as not giving up. And rather than trying to understand everything, it simply says, "Lord, I trust you."

THE BASIS OF OUR FAITH

If we base our faith on our feelings, we're asking for a roller-coaster ride, and on bad days that can be a terrible trip. And the ride takes us nowhere but in circles—a double bummer. If we base our faith on our intellect, we chain our faith to only what we understand

and accept. That's like handcuffing ourselves to a stake, because the very nature of faith takes us beyond what we can explain.

Kenneth Hagin, who inspired many to faith in the last century, said, "To believe with all your heart is to believe independently of your head and [the feelings] of your body. . . . If you want to walk by faith, the Word must be superior to anything and everything else. It must be superior to any knowledge, whether that knowledge is yours or someone else's."[4] This is the point at which a person steps out in faith and may be called crazy by others. Some people really are crazy or misguided— and fail. But if we're led by God and humbly base our trust on him and his Word, we will start seeing answers and miracles that we otherwise would not.

Living by faith may seem irrational. Actually, it is. It goes beyond reason. Faith believes *before* it sees and sometimes believes *contrary* to what it sees. "We live by faith, not by sight" (2 Cor. 5:7). To believe only after we see is merely to acknowledge a result. Jesus promises nothing when we merely acknowledge results, only when we believe. Hebrews 11:1 says simply, "Faith is being sure of what we hope for and certain of what we do not see." Whether we're brand-new believers or PhD-toting theologians, faith is basically simple: we trust God. The hard part is being willing.

GIVE FAITH A VISION

Though faith believes what it cannot yet see, it sometimes needs a vision to hold on to. That vision can be a dream or a clear idea of a goal. A great Old Testament man of God, Abram (before his name changed to Abraham), was bummed out. He and his wife were old, with no hope of having kids. So God took him out to stargaze. God gave him a vision, a picture image, to inspire his faith. In Genesis 15:5 God essentially says, "Count the stars if you can, Abe. You'll have that many descendants." So "Abram believed the Lord" (v. 6), and the Lord considered him righteous for it. And he got the kid, followed by countless descendants.

Jesus invites us to believe a vision into reality when he says, "If anyone says to this mountain, 'Go, throw yourself into the sea,' and does not doubt in his heart but believes that what he says will happen, it will be done for him" (Mark 11:23). I used to wonder how to apply a verse like that. Then I thought of the back problems I'd had since junior high—I knew the chiropractor's office like my own house. I replaced "mountain" with "backbone" and said to my back, "Be straightened." I prayed that prayer many times and resisted the temptation to think I was being silly. My back improved. I still trust in the truth of that verse when I pray for my back, and I almost never go to the chiropractor anymore.

Any problem or challenge you face could be that "mountain," and God is in the moving business.

PRAYER
~ *Starter* ~

Lord, may the challenges I face cause my faith to rise up. I believe your Word and trust you. Move me to trust you more. . . .

A Growing
Heart

— DAY 6 —

CLEANING HOUSE

When Kim and I were missionaries in Japan, she spent some time in the States taking care of relatives and people getting married. I was alone on the other side of the Pacific Ocean. Her two-and-a-half-month stay felt like an eternity. When a guy is lonely long enough, he sometimes does things he normally wouldn't do. I went out and bought a porno magazine. I hate pornography. I cringe at how it attracted me. And I'm ashamed that I leered at it. It made me shrink and feel dirty and reduced me to, as the Bible says, "a loaf of bread" (Prov. 6:26). I felt eaten—by lust and by loneliness. I hate when the devil is happy.

At the same time I had the flu as well as a sinus infection that wouldn't go away. No matter how much I prayed and believed God for healing, the infection wouldn't heal. And the medicine didn't do much either. Then Kim called. I confessed, told her everything. She said she understood. She forgave me and prayed for me. That was one of those moments when I knew she was truly a Christian. I ripped up the magazine and threw it out.

Immediately, one of those things that almost never happens, happened. The pain from the infection decreased about 75 percent. And my whole body, soul, and spirit started coming back to life. It was as if someone pulled the sickness right out of me.

I share this because sometimes the critical difference in answered prayer—and in our entire lives—is cleaning house. We are temples of God's Spirit (1 Cor. 3:16), and like any other place, temples need to be cleaned. We aren't really cleaning a house if we sweep dirt under the carpets and throw pretty sheets over piles of trash. Too many of us do that kind of thing with our personal lives when we cover up and pretend that everything's fine. Whether cleaning our house or our personal lives, we can't genuinely do it without being honest—with God and sometimes with others.

THE BURDEN OF SIN AND THE FREEDOM OF REPENTANCE

The burden of unconfessed sin shows itself in spiritual lethargy, emotional turmoil, and sometimes physical illness. In Psalm 32:3–5 King David groaned:

> When I kept silent,
>> my bones wasted away
>> through my groaning all day long.
> For day and night
>> your hand was heavy upon me;
>> my strength was sapped
>> as in the heat of summer.
> Then I acknowledged my sin to you
>> and did not cover up my iniquity.
>> I said, "I will confess
>> my transgressions to the LORD"—
>> and you forgave
>> the guilt of my sin.

Was he ever miserable. And God let him be. God will let us be miserable too, if that's what it takes for us to get right with him. He loves us and hurts with us through whatever is necessary to turn us back to him.

When I was a kid and my mother spanked me, I remember looking up and seeing tears in her eyes. All I was thinking about was my sore butt. Her tears shocked me. It had not occurred to me that she would hurt too. I suspect God is like that: rather than snarling and holding a stick, he more likely has tears in his eyes. And like the father in the parable of the prodigal son, he spreads his hands to embrace us.

Bernard of Clairvaux, the great twelfth-century monastic leader, grasped the essence of God's conviction of sin that leads us to his mercy: "When [people] are distressed to see what they are, they long to be what they are not, and fear that they will never be by their own efforts. . . . Since they see that they cannot do it by themselves . . . they fly from justice to mercy."[1] We can do a lot by our own effort, but when we want to get right with God, it's time to plead his mercy.

Throughout history, in all expressions of the Christian church, confession has been among the first orders of prayer. And no wonder. How can we connect with God if we've got sin stiff-arming him away from us? He will hardly even hear us.

THE LORD'S DEAF EAR

I've heard people who live openly selfish and sinful lifestyles complain that God didn't answer their prayers. They didn't like to hear Psalm 66:18, which says, "If I had cherished sin in my heart, the Lord would not have listened." Similarly, the prophet Isaiah rebukes Israel, saying, "Surely the arm of the LORD is not too short to save, nor his ear too dull to hear. But your iniquities have separated you from your God; your sins have hidden his face from you, so that he will not hear" (Isa. 59:1–2). If that's true, God literally refuses to listen to us when we knowingly pray with unconfessed sin. That's something to stop and think about.

There seem to be at least two reasons for this. One is that God is holy and has no fellowship with anything unholy. If we wallow in sin, we'll lose intimacy with God, because he will have nothing to do with our sin. We're still saved, but our sin distances us from him. Another reason is that if he answered us in the midst of our sinning, it would suggest that it's okay to go on with unconfessed sin, that God doesn't mind. We would therefore sink our lives ever deeper into our sin and all its consequences.

Withholding answers to prayer may be one of God's ways of keeping us right with him.

SIN — WHETHER WE MEAN IT OR NOT

One definition of sin is a willful violation of a known law of God. That's the we-have-no-excuse kind of infringement—we know better but still violate God's law. The end result of making this a habit does not look good: Hebrews 10:26–27 says, "If we deliberately keep on sinning after we have received the knowledge of the truth," the only thing we have to look forward to is "a fearful expectation of judgment and of raging fire." Ouch. In the Old Testament people didn't have to wait so long. Intentional, defiant sin usually meant being stoned to death or cut off from the rest of the people (Num. 15:30–31).

Another definition of sin is anything that "fall[s] short of the glory of God" (Rom. 3:23). That's the we-have-no-escape kind of infringement—anyone who is breathing is guilty. Most people don't read Leviticus a lot, but chapters 4 and 5 explain sacrifices required for forgiveness "when anyone sins unintentionally and does what is forbidden in any of the LORD's commands" (4:1). It's like when a police officer pulls us over and we say we didn't know the speed limit, but he tells us it's posted somewhere so we're guilty anyway. Whenever we violate a command of Scripture, even if we're unaware that we've done so, it is sin.

However we sin, the Bible says we must deal with it, without rationalizing or making excuses. So we confess everything—what we know and what we don't. God is serious about sin because it degrades us and separates us from him. For a healthy relationship, I recommend a contrite heart, a heart ready to repent or grieve over sin (Isa. 66:2). Contrite hearts receive lots of mercy.

KEEP RIGHT WITH GOD AND OTHERS—FORGIVE

My wife and I knew a couple who I thought were exemplary Christians. But they didn't receive many answers to prayer. Often new people who were less mature in their faith came to the church and received sometimes miraculous answers to prayer, and they talked publicly about the great things God did in their lives. And so this couple only grew more frustrated. "Why always them and not us?" they would grumble.

We were baffled. But as time passed, the reason became clear. This couple held grudges against people who acted wrongly toward them, and they justified it by saying they had greater faith than those who wronged them. ("I have greater faith"—what a rationale for justifying unforgiveness.) When others received answers to prayer, they held grudges against those people and even against God. The downward spiral got worse until they finally left the church.

To maintain a healthy relationship with God, we have no choice but to regularly forgive others. Unforgiveness is a particularly nasty problem. Jesus wants to make sure we don't get stuck in it, so forgiving is the only part of the Lord's Prayer that he reiterates (Matt. 6:14–15). He says that if we forgive others, our heavenly Father will forgive us, but if we don't forgive others, the Father will not forgive us either. Walking around unforgiven all the time is a terrible burden.

It gets worse. Paul indicates that Satan schemes through human unforgiveness. In 2 Corinthians 2:10–11 Paul says that he forgives anything that needs to be forgiven, "in order that Satan might not outwit us. For we are not unaware of his schemes." Likewise he tells us in Ephesians 4:26–27, "'In your anger do not sin': Do not let the sun go down while you are still angry, and do not give the devil a foothold." Unforgiveness is the devil's open door.

I often hear people say, "I can't forgive. They don't deserve it!" They're right—they don't deserve it. Nor do we. But God will deal with them, as he will with us. Romans 12:19 promises, "'It is mine to avenge; I will repay,' says the Lord." Do we trust God enough to let him take care of justice?

I have found that we forgive people not because they deserve it; we forgive because we are called to be like Jesus. We forgive others as he forgave us, and we leave judgment to the Father. When we do, he is glorified—and he reflects his glory back to us.

We also forgive others not for their sake but for our own. We forgive in order to set ourselves free. When others are not sorry for wrongs they have done to us, it doesn't matter. We forgive them for *our* sake, because unforgiveness builds a spiritual prison. Forgiveness is the key that unlocks that prison. When you forgive someone, you set a prisoner free. Then you realize the prisoner was you. That's probably why God commands us to forgive. He knows the bondage that occurs when we don't forgive and the release that occurs when we do.

Forgiveness is an extraordinary act.

TAKING IT FURTHER — GET FORGIVEN

Jesus takes it one step further, when he says to be reconciled if "your brother has something against you" (Matt. 5:23), not "if you have something against your brother." You might be totally unaware of having done anything wrong. But Jesus says that if someone else has something against you, "leave your gift there in front of the altar. First go and be reconciled to your brother, then come and offer your gift" (v. 24). Whether we are right or wrong is not the issue. We'd do best to forget about who's right or wrong. We need to reconcile. Whether with God or with others, the important thing—worth any price—is to be in a right relationship.

PRAYER
~ *Starter* ~

Lord, you know my heart, and you know what I have done and have not done. I repent of [name the sin], and I receive your forgiveness. I also choose to leave judgment in your hands and forgive those who have wronged me. Keep me right with you and with others. . . .

— DAY 7 —

CHARACTER GROWTH

The 1993 movie *Shadowlands* portrays C. S. Lewis's life with Joy Gresham and her struggle with cancer. For a time she goes into remission and all seems hopeful. As Lewis and his Oxford colleagues prepare to enter Magdalene College chapel, Harry, the vicar, affirms him: "I know how hard you've been praying. Now God is answering your prayer."

Lewis looks blankly ahead and responds, half to Harry, half to himself, "That's not why I pray, Harry. I pray because I can't help myself. I pray because I'm helpless. I pray because the need flows out of me—all the time, waking and sleeping. It doesn't change God; it changes me."[1]

CHOOSE THE PATH THAT MAY HURT

Prayer doesn't change God; it changes us. Lewis went beyond just asking God to answer his prayer. He recognized that as he grew close to God, God would change him and grow him through the pain. The writer of Hebrews asserts that Jesus himself "learned obedience from what he suffered" (5:8) and that he was made "perfect through suffering" (2:10). Similar opportunities knock on our doors. Think of times in your life when pain or hardship helped make you a better person—as when Paul says, "Suffering produces perseverance; perseverance, character; and character, hope" (Rom. 5:3–4). What was the process that brought change? Would you agree that when difficulty leads to growth, it can be worth the ache?

Part of growing Christlike is through pain. Pain is the knife that cuts open our hearts. And Jesus is the surgeon of the soul.

When facing adversity, we're naturally tempted to cry, "God, rescue me!" But if we ask him to save us from our problems, we lose sight of how he meets us in the midst of them—as when David prays in Psalm 23:4, "Even though I walk through the valley of the shadow of death, I will fear no evil, for you are with me." Hardship is probably the most common tool God uses to grow our character. C. S. Lewis says, "God whispers to us in our pleasures, speaks in our conscience, but shouts in our pains: it is his megaphone to rouse a deaf world."[2]

Sometimes it's God's will for us to endure trouble. That's when we wake up enough to pay attention to what he can do in our lives. It's no surprise that Christians who face persecution are often so spiritually alive—the constant adversity drives them closer to God.

Brace yourself when you ask God to increase your faith or when you ask him to make you more Christlike. His answer to that kind of prayer tends to involve pain.

INVITE GOD IN

Asaph, the temple-praise-team guy who wrote Psalm 73, was in the dumps. Frustrated that wicked people lived in comfort and power while he struggled, he started the psalm with bitterness, self-pity, moaning, and bellyaching. As we read through the psalm, we find that the wicked didn't change, but he did. In verses 21–26 we see the turn:

> When my heart was grieved
>   and my spirit embittered,
> I was senseless and ignorant;
>   I was a brute beast before you.
> Yet I am always with you;
>   you hold me by my right hand.
> You guide me with your counsel,
>   and afterward you will take me into glory.
> Whom have I in heaven but you?
>   And earth has nothing I desire besides you.
> My flesh and my heart may fail,
>   but God is the strength of my heart
>   and my portion forever.

We won't find more honesty than "I was a brute beast." At times I've felt that was me, and I've prayed those words along with Asaph. Instead of avoiding God in his misery, Asaph admitted that he stood before God and with God, and that God held him, guided him, and would give him hope for the future. From verse 3, "I envied the arrogant when I saw the prosperity of the wicked," to verse 25, "earth has nothing I desire besides you," we see a total transformation of his attitude. Like Asaph, my own thinking has often transformed from critical to hopeful, and my feelings from bitterness to peace with God. My situations did not always change. But I did.

We can ask God to change other people. Yet God gives humans a lot of room to buck. We are given authority over the spirit world, but we are not given authority over other people's beliefs, attitudes, or behaviors. So if we're praying for others to change, patience will come in handy. Sometimes people may be sensitive enough to respond to the Holy Spirit, and sometimes they may be hardened enough that they never respond. But no matter what they do or don't do, we will find that *we* change. We get closer to God, which leads us to understand ourselves differently and grow in character.

A young woman, whom I'll call Cindy, was married to a guy who continually argued, drank, smoked, stayed out all night, and could hardly hold a job. She prayed long and hard for him to change. He didn't—but she did. She quit trying to change him and asked God to deal with him. Cindy grew to become one of the most Christlike people I have ever met. Instead of changing Cindy's husband, God changed her. And that in turn began a change in her husband.

Things change when God is unleashed in a person's heart. I wanted to be both a writer and a pastor. Then God told me to stop writing. I didn't want to hear that. He kept telling me, and I couldn't escape it. For months I resisted. I felt the Spirit hound my thoughts and my feelings until finally I gave up my desire. For more than two years I wrote nothing but class notes, term papers, and checks. Then one December night, I sensed the Holy Spirit, as clear as if he were standing next to me, telling me to start writing again.

What was that all about? I concluded that God knew my desire to write was selfish, carnal, and unbaptized. During those two-plus years, God was changing me. When I aligned myself with him and the time was right, he gave back my desire—along with his calling.

My guess is that you may have had a similar experience. Or you will. I've learned to lower my resistance to God when I suspect he wants to change me. When I say yes to change, whatever price I pay is always worth it.

Change happens in small ways too. Many times I catch myself worrying. Then I pray, and the very act of praying changes my attitude. Anxiety turns to peace. Fear turns to faith. Stress turns to comfort. Everything changes when it finds its way into God's hands.

KEEP PRAYER IN BALANCE

Asking God for things—the fancy word is *supplication*—is just one part of prayer. More of us acknowledge this than practice it. We tend to ask more than we thank, praise, confess, or meditate *combined.* The frequently used ACTS (or CATS) acronym (Adoration, Confession, Thanksgiving, Supplication) reminds us of our prayer priorities. Most of the prayers in the Bible are also in harmony with this pattern. It helps us communicate with God more comprehensively than we could with a give-me list. Praising and confessing and thanking may take practice. But when we do those things, the entire nature of our prayers changes.

Here's a question to ask yourself: "If I knew that I would not get any of the things I asked from God, would I still pray?" If you pray mainly in order to *get*—even to get good things—you are missing the main reason to pray. The main thing is to connect with God, to be with him. Similar to spending time with a person you love, when you spend time with God, you become more like him. Here's the bonus: when you're more like him, you pray more in line with his will, and you receive more answers to the things you ask.

If you want God to change you, offer yourself as what the Bible calls "a living sacrifice" (Rom. 12:1), a life given over to God, inviting God in and letting go of things that get in the way of a healthy spiritual life. The result, expressed in the next verse, is the wonderful experience of mind renewal. I've experienced this as my nasty tendencies have gradually been "transformed by the renewing of [my] mind" (v. 2). I hope you experience it too—this mind-set that grows in harmony with God.

DAILY DISCIPLINE

If we eat right, exercise, and rest, we'll probably have healthy bodies. If we eat junk food, never exercise, and rarely rest, that will show too. It's the same with our spiritual nature. If we don't talk to God much, the results will show in how we relate to him and others. For me, if I don't spend much time with God for two days in a row, I don't even want to be around myself. People who are kind and sweet by nature may get by longer than ornery people. But whatever our personality, we'll shortchange ourselves (and others) without prayer.

Paul, who continually prayed for his churches, prays for the Ephesians in chapter 1 of his letter to them, that they will receive enlightenment to know who they are in Christ (v. 18). He doesn't assume they'll change; he yearns that change will be real for them. In chapter 3 he prays that they will be strengthened and receive the fullness of God (vv. 16, 19). These are two of the longest prayer summaries in the New Testament, and they focus on character change.

The act of praying infuses our thinking with God's presence. As the mind of God permeates our own minds on a regular basis, it changes our overall thinking, feeling, and behaving. When we pray, we cannot help but connect with God himself.

PRAYER
~ Starter ~

God, change me. I submit myself to whatever it takes. May your Spirit work deep within me to heal, correct, and transform me from the inside out. . . .

—— *DAY 8* ——

PRAISE POWER

When Kim and I were starting new churches in Japan, I taught at a college to help support us. One of my American teaching colleagues was disgruntled with God. She was disgruntled with life altogether. She often heard me hum a worship song or say, "Praise God!" That bothered her—not just my praising but the fact that the Bible tells us to praise God at all.

One afternoon she furrowed her brow at me. "Why does God always want people to worship him?" She paused, apparently to let the gravity of her feelings sink in. "What's his problem? Does he have such a weak ego that he needs people to bow down to him all the time?"

I stared at her for a few seconds. "Good question."

A very good question. Too often believers praise and worship God because they grew up doing it or because everyone else does it on Sunday morning. And they don't ask why.

It would be easy to say we worship God because he is God—and leave it at that. What else would we rightly do before the Creator and Master of the universe? Philippians 2 makes it clear that Jesus' name (which represents his authority) is above all others and that "at the name of Jesus every knee should bow, in heaven and on earth and under the earth" (v. 10). All those in heaven, on earth, and in hell will bow, whether by choice now or by force later. That's all true. Yet there's more. My colleague's question motivated me to find it.

THE BIGGEST ISSUE IN THE UNIVERSE

Most people aren't used to hearing this, but worship is the biggest issue in the universe.[1] Yes, worship. Yes, the entire universe. Whoever receives worship is a higher authority than the one who worships. Worship acknowledges who or what has that authority. Believers of every faith have implicitly recognized this through the centuries. The ancient Celtic church understood this, as we see in one of their major hymns, "Patrick's Breastplate" (as in St. Patrick), from around the eighth century:

> I bind unto myself the name,
> The strong name of the Trinity,
> By invocation of the same,
> The three in one, and One in Three,

Of whom all nature has creation;
Eternal Father, Spirit, Word,
Praise to the Lord of my salvation
Salvation is of Christ the Lord.[2]

In this hymn we see the Celts' strong belief in God, the Lord of the universe and of their souls. And they praise him. The first line expresses their sense of personal intimacy with God. It's no wonder the Celts were among the most spiritually alive and fervent Christians in church history.

It should also be no surprise that Satan's main effort throughout human history has been to exalt himself and be worshiped, whether directly through Satanism or indirectly through sin. We catch a glimpse of this in Isaiah 14:12–14, which describes Satan's arrogant desire to raise himself above God. The "morning star," which is *Lucifer* in Latin, schemes to "ascend to heaven," to raise his throne "above the stars of God," and to "sit enthroned ... on the utmost heights ... like the Most High." By distracting and perverting people's attention, Satan steals the reverence they would otherwise give to God. Every form of ungodliness is ultimately a part of Satan's desire to be worshiped or at least weaken our worship of God.

When we praise and worship God, it has cosmic implications. Worshipers give authority and dominion to the one they worship. This act and its result, by definition, constitute a kingdom. Outside the human realm, there are ultimately only two kingdoms: God's and Satan's. In the end there will be only one.

Terry Law observes that "God is always king whether we praise Him or not. . . . But when we praise Him we offer Him a throne to sit upon in *our* presence. That is why our praise is so necessary in order to bring *the power of the presence of God*" into our lives.[3] So Jesus is Lord over the universe, but where it matters to us is whether we acknowledge that he is Lord over our personal lives.

The central blessing we receive is this: as we ascribe glory to God, he in turn shares his glory with us. Second Corinthians 3:18 says that we "reflect the Lord's glory." This can occasionally happen in overpowering, supernatural ways that we call revival. More commonly, the Holy Spirit blesses us with joy, encouragement, or renewed faith. When we give glory to God, he is pleased to share his glory with us. We experience that in two big ways: he lifts us up, and he becomes to us what we praise him for.

LIFTED TO A HIGHER LEVEL

Praising God lifts us from where we're at to a higher level. Psalm 40:2 says it well: "He lifted me out of the slimy pit, out of the mud and mire; he set my feet on a rock and gave me a firm place to stand."

How often have you been in a less-than-happy mood when you walked into a worship service? I was when my mom hauled me to church as a boy. I was a Boy Scout, and Boy Scouts were supposed to be honest. So when I was less than happy (which was most of the time), I figured it was a virtue to sit through the whole worship service as sour as a pickle.

Later in life I discovered that the most genuine praise of God rises not out of feelings but out of faith, regardless of how we feel. Praising God when we get healed or receive lots of money is simply an appropriate response. But willfully praising God when we are discouraged or in trouble is an act of faith. Acts of faith are more genuine than acts of feeling, because they rise from the heart and not from circumstances. As hard as it may be in tough times, deliberately praising God is the best thing we can do for ourselves.

When I was a young Christian, I was deeply in love with a woman who decided to dump me. I sank into depression and cried buckets of tears. One day I consoled my pitiful self by singing praise songs I had learned in church. A half hour into it I stopped in surprise. Sometime during that time, my tears of sadness over lost love had turned into tears of joy over love found in Jesus. The act of praising God lifted me up and changed me.

Praising God sometimes comes as naturally as breathing. Other times it's a struggle—then it's time to crank the engine. I clench my teeth and praise God out of sheer determination. It's a funny sight to see: a droopy-dog face praising Jesus. I do it because each time, the act of my will gradually leads into a natural flow of praise. My teeth unclench, and my face brightens.

GOD BECOMES TO US WHAT WE PRAISE HIM FOR

When we praise God, he becomes to us what we praise him for. In the Psalms we see dozens of ways the Lord relates to us: he is our rock (18:2), our fortress (59:16–17), our deliverer (40:17), our strength (28:7), our healer (30:2), our shepherd (23:1), our joy (43:4), our peace (29:11), our hope (71:5), and our guide (48:14). We declare by faith who God is to us and what he has done for us. When we praise God, we superimpose words and ideas from Scripture over our own thoughts—the way that one photographic image can be laid over another. Joy is superimposed over discouragement. Faith is superimposed over doubt. The lordship of Christ is superimposed over material desires. When these things happen, our thoughts line up with God's thoughts, and our praise becomes a path on which he meets us.

I used to moan a lot to God. I lamented how sad I was, how sick I was, how poor I was. I didn't know why God seemed to leave me sad, sick, and poor. Then I discovered that he responded more to my acknowledgment of who he is than to my begging. One is an act of faith, the other a mere solicitation.

When I'm discouraged I deliberately praise God for being my joy, and without fail, he becomes joy to me. When I'm sick I praise God for being my healer, and many times I experience his touch. When I'm broke I praise God for being my provider, and sometimes I don't know where all the money comes from. It may sound simplistic, but it works, because we're free to choose our attitudes about any situation.

God seems to place no limit on what he will do in response to our praise. In 2 Chronicles 20 King Jehoshaphat was scared to death by the imminent attack of three enemy armies. God told him don't worry, just march out—and, by the way, put the praise team in front. I read this and think, *That's insane.* But God is into crazy things. That's how he tests our faith. So how did he respond? "As they began to sing and praise, the LORD set ambushes" against the enemy (v. 22), and Jehoshaphat won. So no matter what our challenges may be, when we choose to praise God anyway, he becomes to us what we praise him for.

ENJOY

Did you know that it's okay to enjoy your time with your heavenly Father? Experienced intercessors know this. It's part of what keeps them going, and they love to spend time with God. I think sometimes we get so religious that we forget to enjoy God. Many believers think of prayer as a solemn ritual. Prayer is a serious thing, but God never asks us to be solemn. Solemnity is a big part of being religious, and being religious gets in the way of connecting with God.

Styles of praise have changed throughout the centuries, from Gregorian chants to rock bands. Styles vary across cultures and church affiliations. Whether we sing songs or just speak our feelings, God hears it all. The only essential ingredient is a genuine heart.

So let loose. Laugh, shout, and dance in God's presence—he likes it. And he loves you.

PRAYER
~ *Starter* ~

Lord, despite my circumstance [name it], I choose to praise you. You are above my challenges. And as I praise you, I believe that you will lift me up and become to me what I praise you for. . . .

—— DAY 9 ——

SPIRIT LED

Shortly after Kim and I were married, I was recommended to go to India for a two-month mission trip. Kim prayed about it and sensed the Holy Spirit saying I should go.

I laughed. We had no money for a trip like that.

A few days later while looking at a world map, I felt over-whelmed by a sense of people dying and going into an eternity separated from God. I had a weird vision in which a screw bored through me, lifted me up, and landed me on a map of India. Maybe God was telling me something.

People started donating money right and left. I was astounded that within two weeks I received more than $2,000—airfare plus $400 for expenses.

Then Kim used $1,600 of it to pay the rent for a widow who was about to be evicted from her home. I appreciated Kim's mercy yet wondered if it was a misappropriation of funds—or if helping the widow had been God's intent from the start.

With the departure date only three weeks away, I decided to give up the trip and work as a painter on a maintenance crew. The next day I was playing racquetball and sensed the Holy Spirit say to me, *You're standing safely in the back of this racquetball court just as you do in the back court of your life. You need to step forward in faith.* Maybe God still wanted me to go.

A few days later, we came home to find a friend of Kim's waiting for us outside our apartment. She said, "Whenever I pray I feel that the Holy Spirit is telling me to pay your air ticket." She handed us a check for $1,600.

I went to India—and the entire time Kim prayed for me every night in the church sanctuary. The time I spent in India was the most spiritually intense period of my entire life, and the fruit was abundant: many pastors were trained, believers were encouraged, and 127 people were baptized.

I learned that when the Holy Spirit leads, he leads no matter what. We're wise to follow.

PRAYING IN THE SPIRIT

Paul tells us in Ephesians 6:18 to "pray in the Spirit on all occasions." Jude 20 tells us to "pray in the Holy Spirit." I often wondered what that phrase meant, so I looked it up. The Greek word in these verses is typically translated "in" but can also mean "by" or "with." Some people debate the differences, but there really aren't any. We can take our pick and pray "in," "with," or "by" the Holy Spirit.

Think of it like driving a car. Praying in the Spirit means that we get out of the driver's seat of our prayer lives and let the Spirit steer. It means we open our minds and hearts and yield to the Spirit's prompting in what we pray. To do this, it helps to slow down and quiet ourselves. Praying in the Spirit can include at least three things: seeking the Holy Spirit and letting him lead our prayer (Rom. 8:26; Eph. 6:18); being empowered by the Holy Spirit (James 5:16); or praying with our spirit, as Paul describes in terms that equate it with tongues (1 Cor. 14:14–15).

Time for a disclaimer: praying in the Spirit can be a controversial subject. Doctrine and experience can divide believers. And people too often base their doctrine on experience. Some might think, *Spirit led? That means praying in tongues.* Others will think, *Spirit led? That means God is leading and we don't know it.* I'm convinced that the full truth goes beyond any one position. However you understand the Holy Spirit's work in your life, pray in the Spirit. If you're Pentecostal or charismatic, then pray fervently in the Spirit as you know it. If you're noncharismatic, then pray fervently in the Spirit in the way you know how. Until we get to heaven, let's be as accepting of each other as God is of us.

APPROACHES TO PRAYING IN THE SPIRIT

Let's take a look at three possibilities when praying in the Spirit.

Seeking the Holy Spirit and letting him lead our prayer. However we may interpret praying in the Spirit, it begins with giving up our own control and yielding our minds and wills to the Lord. Any other way is definitively not "in the Spirit." Romans 8:26 clarifies it: "The Spirit helps us in our weakness. We do not know what we ought to pray for, but the Spirit himself intercedes for us with groans that words cannot express." Praying in the Spirit acknowledges our human weakness and our dependency on God when we try to connect with him and pray effectively.

Being empowered by the Holy Spirit. A literal translation of James 5:16 is, "The energized prayer of a righteous one is very powerful." The Greek word used for "energized" (*energeo*) relates primarily to supernatural activity. So it might read, "The supernaturally energized prayer of a righteous person is very powerful." In this sense, praying in the Spirit means that our prayer is empowered, or energized, by the Spirit. If you've ever been energized like this, or you've been with others who were, you need no further explanation. If not, make a note that empowerment can mean increased energy in prayer and increased supernatural answers to prayer.

Praying with our spirit. In 1 Corinthians 14:14–15 Paul explains, "If I pray in a tongue, my spirit prays, but my mind is unfruitful. So what shall I do? I will pray with my spirit, but I will also pray with my mind." This passage expresses the place of the human spirit in prayer. Who does our spirit connect with in prayer? The Holy Spirit. When we pray in the Spirit, our spirit connects with God. Here when talking about private prayer, Paul uses the term *tongues* differently from the more distinct gift of tongues (12:10) and the admonition to have interpretation when speaking in tongues publicly (14:27). Here tongues are exercised in prayer or singing rather than as a message to the church. And judging by the context of verses 2, 9, and 16, it sounds more like incoherent utterances than a discernable language as it does in Acts 2:5–12. Overall, we would be wise to follow Paul's general counsel in 1 Corinthians 14 to neither overemphasize tongues on one hand nor forbid them on the other (vv. 18–19, 39).

I am often awed at how generous and embracing the Holy Spirit is toward us who have limited, yet diverse, understandings of his ways.

An Underused Blessing

Praying in the Spirit seems to be ignored. Many people are unsure of how, or even if, the Spirit leads us. And some of us are afraid of yielding to the Holy Spirit—it's scary not to be in control.

Engines need oil to keep them running smoothly, whether they're idling or racing. Praying in the Spirit is like oil in an engine. It maintains continuity and momentum whether we are saying anything in particular or not. We don't stop and start but rather continue in an attitude of prayer. When we pause, it's to wait on the Lord—not because we've run out of words and are trying to think of what to pray next.

If the Spirit leads our prayer, we have freedom to wait on the Lord because we're intentionally letting his Spirit lead us. We no longer feel obligated to always talk, then quit when we're done. We can quietly pause and follow the Spirit's leading. When we sense his leading, we pray with greater confidence than we ever could by our own direction.

One summer the Holy Spirit prompted me to pray for "one lost or wandering soul"—that is, one person, or family, who was not a believer or was a believer but not associated with any church—to come into the kingdom of God every month. At the time we had thirty to forty people on an average Sunday. Because the prompting was so clear, I prayed with great faith. I kept records from that month forward and found that almost every month God sovereignly led people to faith through our church.

PRAYING BY THE SPIRIT'S LEADING

From their beginnings in the seventeenth century until today, the Quakers (also known as the Friends Church) have emphasized waiting on God and following the Spirit's guidance. They do this both individually and corporately. According to their tradition, worship "is entirely without any human direction or supervision. A group of devout persons come together and sit down quietly with no prearrangement, each seeking to have an immediate sense of divine leading and to know at first hand the presence of the Living Christ."[1] Under the leadership of their founder, George Fox, "they simply *gathered, listened, waited,* and sought to be *obedient.*"[2]

If you have never prayed this way, try it. Quietly sitting and listening for the Holy Spirit's guidance takes practice and getting used to, but doing so could lead you into a whole new dimension of praying in the will and power of God.

If you're unsure of whether or not you have the Spirit's leading, wait until you sense a repeated thought, feeling, or mental impression. Give yourself the benefit of the doubt. God loves you and knows that you are doing your best to discern what he is communicating. The more you yield to the Spirit, the more your discernment will grow. Let what you hear from God be tentative. Test it. And pray with confidence.

Take some encouragement from baseball. When a professional bats over 300, he's considered to be very good. But that means he only makes a hit three out of ten times at bat. So don't beat yourself up when you miss.

PRAYER
～ *Starter* ～

Lord, I yield myself to you; guide me as I seek you. Lead me and empower me, especially when I don't know how to pray. . . .

— *DAY 10* —

PRACTICING GOD'S
PRESENCE

Nicholas Herman, known by his lay monastic name, Brother Lawrence, was a soldier, a footman, and an unsuccessful hermit (he couldn't stand living alone) before he became a cook in a Carmelite monastery in Paris in the mid-seventeenth century. We hardly know anything about him, except that he was the first to articulate the concept and lifestyle of continually practicing the presence of God. This was an uneducated guy who cooked and washed dishes. He participated in the monastery's prayer and worship, but he also chopped onions, swept the floor, and went to the market with an intimate and continual awareness of God's presence. Preferring anonymity, he never published anything. But he wrote in a letter, "I make it my only business to persevere in His holy Presence, wherein I keep myself by a simple attention and an absorbing passionate regard to God, which I may call an actual Presence of God."[1] Joseph de Beaufort, the only one to ever formally interview him, wrote, "His prayer was nothing else but a sense of the presence of God, his soul being at that time insensible to everything but divine love; and that when the appointed times of prayer were past, he found no difference, because he still continued with God."[2]

PRACTICING THE PRESENCE

God is omnipresent, which means he is everywhere all the time. So wherever we go, God is there. Practicing the presence of God moves beyond acknowledging some theological truth to actually experiencing it. Like Brother Lawrence, we focus our attention on God and recognize that he is always with us, and we are with him.

Moses understood the significance of God's constant presence when he pleaded, "If your Presence does not go with us, do not send us up from here" (Exod. 33:15). God's presence to him and all the Israelites meant that God would be their protector and provider. Directly or indirectly, God is the source of meeting whatever need we have.

The main benefit of practicing the presence of God is not to haul in the good things he offers. It is to connect with God himself. The intimacy of his Spirit is the greatest reward. As we practice awareness of him, we naturally receive good things from him, but those things become secondary to uniting with God himself. The sons of Korah express in Psalm 84:10 that abiding in God's presence is better than having a high, worldly position: "I would rather be a doorkeeper in the house of my God than dwell in the tents of the wicked." They're not asking anything of God; they want only *him*.

If we're practicing the presence of God, rather than spending time with God and then going off to a busy day, we develop a continual sense that he is with us in all things throughout the day. Brother Lawrence gave the example that "reaching down to the ground to get a straw, if done to show love to God, made him happy."[3] Paul agrees in his first letter to the Corinthians: "Whether you eat or drink or whatever you do, do it all for the glory of God" (10:31). This verse tells us that literally *anything*, however small, can be done to the glory of God.

Along with me, you might ask, "How do we do this?" Paul tells us to "pray continually" (1 Thess. 5:17). I think Douglas Steere comes close to explaining this when he assesses Brother Lawrence's words and says that he does not mean "we should or could pray vocally continuously, or that we could consciously think of God constantly. But we can so fix our will and our affections upon God as to permeate all that we do with this relationship."[4] It means we're always aware that God is with us, ready to see him anywhere in anything, attentive to how he might communicate to us, always loving him and ready to praise him. This closely relates to hunger for God and intimacy with God. But here we take that hunger and intimacy into everyday life, even into all its mundane details.

That said, one kind of prayer can come close to being continual.

BREATH PRAYERS

Breath prayers are short prayers that can be said with one breath. They are often repeated in order to keep attention on God. The oldest breath prayer around has been known for centuries as the "Jesus Prayer." Developed at least as early as the fifth century with Diadochus of Photike, a bishop in northern Greece, it is widely used among Eastern, Roman, and Protestant churches today: "Lord Jesus Christ, Son of God, have mercy on me" (some churches add, "a sinner"). The Gospels tell of blind men and lepers who begged for healing, the Canaanite woman who pleaded for her daughter's healing, and Jesus' parable of the tax collector in the temple. All of them cried out for mercy. All of them received it.

A breath prayer is repeated throughout the day to help calm the heart and mind in order to focus on God. It is not the repetitious babbling that Jesus denounced in Matthew 6:7. Rather it is a continual prayer from the heart meant to permeate our consciousness by humble intimacy with Jesus. It's nothing magical, but it has been a way countless Christians have grown closer to the Lord.

If you're like me and prefer something more spontaneous, pray according to your need: "Cleanse my heart, Lord." "Fill me with your Spirit." "I receive your peace." "I trust you, Lord." "I praise you, Jesus." When I express prayers like these throughout the day, my whole attitude changes for the better.

GOD'S PRESENCE IN LITTLE THINGS

God is in little things. Jesus says, "Even the very hairs of your head are all numbered" (Matt. 10:30). Paul encourages slaves, whose entire lives consisted of menial work, with the words, "Whatever you do, work at it with all your heart, as working for the Lord, not for men" (Col. 3:23). If we treat little things as unworthy of our attention, we miss countless opportunities. One opportunity is to experience God in every part of life, as the verse above implies. Another is to love others through serving them in small ways. Mother Teresa said it well: "In this life we cannot do great things. We can only do small things with great love."[5]

I often do maintenance on our church property. I like manual labor once in a while, and it saves the church money. Many things I delegate, but when I clean, rake, or fix things, I'm occasionally tempted to think I should be doing something more significant. Sometimes that's true. But I've also found that when I do a small task with the love of God in my heart and do it as unto the Lord, the very nature of what I'm doing changes. The task itself doesn't change, but I change, and the task becomes a labor of love.

We can practice God's presence anywhere while doing almost anything. Kim once worked at a motel, where she made lots of beds and cleaned lots of toilets. With each bed, she prayed that the people sleeping there would encounter Christ in their hearts. With each toilet, she prayed that God would clean out the hearts of the people who used it. She really did that. Whether it's doing business, weeding the garden, or taking out the trash, with an awareness of God, any task can take on a new dimension.

Slowing Down and Cutting Down

In most places of the world today, the pace of life is too fast, and schedules are too full. Psychologist Archibald Hart says, "The pace of modern life far exceeds what we were designed for. We were designed for camel travel. But we try to function like supersonic jets."[6] Practicing God's presence requires a calm heart that has emotional space to give him attention. When would-be camel travelers like us live at jet speed, it's no wonder we get stressed out. And when we're stressed out, we can hardly practice God's presence, because stress hijacks our sensibilities and leaves no room for God.

If we think our lives are too stressful, they probably are. And there's no use complaining, because ultimately we make our own choices. Whomever or whatever we allow to control us, will. As believers, the only one that should rule over us is the Lord Jesus. Busy lives often have too many rulers. Changing even one or two things can open up wonderful extra space in life.

Too many of us have subconsciously twisted René Descartes' dictum, "I think, therefore I am," to "I'm busy, therefore I'm worthwhile." I've been guilty too many times of feeling a false sense of importance when I'm busy. As believers, our worth is already established in heaven by the fact that we are God's children. We don't have to strive to be worthy of God. We can't earn worthiness anyway. What we do on earth may increase or decrease our reward in heaven, but our worth is already decided and secure in Christ. You and I are so precious and worthwhile that despite all the bad things we've done, Jesus loves us. We were worth dying for. *You* were worth dying for.

PRACTICAL APPROACHES TO PRACTICING THE PRESENCE

Don't be discouraged if you find practicing God's presence difficult. It is. Frank Laubach, who besides Brother Lawrence is best known for his expressions of practicing God's presence, wrote in his diary on May 14, 1930, how difficult and wonderful it is:

> Oh, this thing of keeping in constant touch with God, of making Him the object of my thought and the companion of my conversations, is the most amazing thing I ever ran across. It is working. I cannot do it even half of a day—not yet, but I believe I shall be doing it some day for the entire day. It is a matter of acquiring a new habit of thought. Now I like the Lord's presence so much that when for a half hour or so He slips out of mind—as He does many times a day—I feel as though I had deserted Him, and as though I had lost something very precious in my life.[7]

Here are some practical aspects of practicing God's presence that can make it more possible to do each day. Which ones are most helpful to you?

- My last thought before I sleep and my first thought when I awake is of the Lord.
- Through the busyness of my day, I have a sense that God is there.
- When I get mad or stressed, I try to see things from God's perspective and put them in his hands.
- When I am lonely or depressed, I turn to prayer and invite God into my sadness.

- When I am waiting for someone, I use that time to pray.
- I do menial tasks with an awareness of God and a heart of love toward God.
- I often have a praise song on my mind as I go through the day.

Practicing the presence of God is challenging, but it's achievable. And its main ingredient is desire. I have no doubt that God looks forward to sharing his presence with you as well.

PRAYER
~ *Starter* ~

Lord, move in me to maintain continual awareness of your presence in my life, at every moment, in everything I do. . . .

INTERNAL
HELPS

— DAY *11* —

A Time to Listen

M̲y good friend Gail is a devoted intercessor. God often communicates to her, even wakes her up at night. Here, in her words, is one of her experiences:

Following the sale of our empty-nested home, we had just settled into a cozy little apartment. Both of our children had married within a six-month period, one in April and one in September. On November 10 at 1:15 a.m., I was awakened and drawn into prayer even before I was aware. The Holy Spirit gave me direction to be prepared and wait. I prayed for each family member, fully alert now and with a strong anticipation of impending need. At 2:00 a.m., the phone rang. Our daughter explained that her new husband had become very sick in the last two hours and was rushed by ambulance to a nearby hospital. He had a terrible headache, but she thought he would be okay. My husband and I asked the Lord what to do. We both received a strong answer: *Go!* We quickly dressed and drove to the hospital. When we arrived, our daughter had just received the news that her husband had a cancerous mass on his brain. She was shaken, crying, and spent. She needed Mom and Dad. God had instructed us in the night watch so that we would be there for her, first in prayer, then in person. Weeks, months, and even years of travailing prayer and heartache followed, but God's presence and faithfulness in trouble is certain.

Gail is the kind of person who has ears to hear from God. She shows that following the Holy Spirit's promptings could save someone's life, bring great comfort to someone, or just be a needed blessing in a hard day.

GETTING ENLIGHTENED

The eighteenth-century rise of rationalism, known as the Enlightenment, rejected traditional political, social, and religious ideas. In their place human reason and especially science were emphasized as the primary means to gain and test knowledge and truth. This way of thinking was unfriendly toward anything supernatural, including prayer, the Holy Spirit, and spiritual experience. From a spiritual standpoint, the era might better be called the "Endarkenment."

Listening to God can be done anywhere at any time, but it is most often done through meditation. Because of the Enlightenment's influence on Western civilization, including the church, meditation fell into disrepute both inside and outside the church—until the rise of postmodernism[1] and present-day interest in spirituality. And because the church has so neglected meditation, it's no surprise that many people have turned to Hindu and Buddhist meditation practices. What a tragedy! Christian history before the eighteenth century boasted lineups of people who practiced and wrote on meditation and intimacy with God. They took seriously the Bible's many exhortations to meditate: Joshua is commanded to "meditate" on God's Word "day and night" (Josh. 1:8). The Psalms say, "We meditate on your unfailing love" (Ps. 48:9), and "I will meditate on all your works" (77:12). Christian meditation is the practice of focusing our minds in order to give exclusive attention to God.

Many believers are so unaware of God's "speaking" that they don't think he talks. Most Western Christians do not realize how much our collective Christian consciousness has been secularized by the eighteenth-century Enlightenment and by the scientific rationalism that followed it and continues today. We may profess Christian faith, but sometimes we live our daily lives as if God were on a permanent vacation. And we'll hear (or make up) all manner of spiritual-sounding reasons why God doesn't do, or won't do, the things the Bible says he does. How can we imagine that a God who loves us would not speak to us? Let's reenlighten ourselves!

HEARING FROM GOD

Jesus said, "My sheep listen to my voice; I know them, and they follow me" (John 10:27). We know his voice by listening. What we "hear" can be a mental impression or prompting from the Holy Spirit. During prayer a person may have a strong feeling, sense, or conviction about something. For some (those more left-brained), mental impressions can be a word or indication that an action should be taken. For others (those more right-brained), a picture image or strong feeling may be how God speaks. And we don't have to get analytical or worry about what we think we're receiving. The Bible simply says, "Test everything. Hold on to the good" (1 Thess. 5:21). When the time comes, trust yourself and trust God.

Most of the time what we hear will be simple stuff—nothing to turn us into Old Testament prophets. For example, one morning I was praying and repeatedly felt the urge to call a young man who I knew was going through a hard time. So I called, but he didn't pick up. I left a message. Later that day he called back and told me how much my message encouraged him. Two *months* later he called again and told me he had saved that same message and replayed it every time he needed encouragement. I was amazed how a simple response to what I sensed was the Holy Spirit's leading yielded so much blessing.

WAYS TO HEAR

Too many times we talk to God and forget to listen. O. Hallesby (yes, he went by "O") compares that with going to the doctor:

Suppose that you sit down and begin to tell him about all your pains and troubles. And then when you have talked a long time, suppose you get up, bid a polite adieu, and leave. What would the doctor think? . . . Most likely he would think that some demented person had been in his consulting room by mistake.

God has multitudes of such patients in His waiting room every day. . . . We go out just as we came in.[2]

We should be different after we talk to the doctor of our souls! When you pray, imagine God as that doctor who is willing to respond. You may not hear right away or every time. But keep listening and you will hear.

We can listen to the Holy Spirit when we begin to pray, to seek God's leading in how to pray in the first place. R. A. Torrey writes: "Nothing can be more foolish in prayer than to rush heedlessly into God's presence and ask the first thing that comes into our mind. When we first come into God's presence we should be silent before Him. . . . We must wait for the Holy Spirit and surrender ourselves to the Spirit. Then, we will pray correctly."[3] Torrey may sound a bit strict, but waiting on God is good advice and can alter the whole nature and direction of our prayer. We'll see more answers too.

Hearing also means receiving what Scripture has to tell us, especially when a word convicts us or jumps off the page at us. The biblical term for this is *rhema*, a precise, spoken word for a specific situation—the Bible in its most personal application. It is the sense that God is speaking personally to us from his written Word. Using the term translated *rhema*, Jesus says that we "live . . . on every word that comes from the mouth of God" (Matt. 4:4), and Paul indicates the power of the Word when he calls it the "sword of the Spirit" (Eph. 6:17). They're not kidding.

A man sat in my living room asking for advice on a big decision he had to make. I suggested he read Philippians 4:6–7 out loud and think about it. He started reading verse 6 about not being anxious and presenting his requests, and when he reached verse 7 about the peace of God guarding his heart and mind, he choked up and started bawling. The Holy Spirit suddenly overwhelmed this guy, just by his reading the Scripture. His eyes practically squirted tears, and his nose started running. It took him two minutes to finish the verse. I didn't have to give him any advice. On that day God changed the course of his life.

God also speaks through spiritual gifts that he has given the church to exercise. First Corinthians 12:7–11 lists prophecy (an immediate message from God through a divinely anointed utterance), words of wisdom (a special ability to understand and perceive what should be done in a given situation), and words of knowledge (a special ability to know the ways of God and his Word, which seems to include divinely communicated understanding of people or situations for ministry purposes). Whatever is communicated through these spiritual gifts, 1 Corinthians 14:29 tells us to "weigh carefully what is said." That's so we don't go shouting "hallelujah" before we know what's for real.

On occasion we may hear—or think we hear—an audible voice. Isaiah 30:21 says, "Your ears will hear a voice behind you, saying, 'This is the way; walk in it.'" I suspect that most of the time we'll hear such a voice inside our heads. But more important than finding its location is discerning whether it is from God, the devil, or our own mind. First John 4:1–3 helps us know: if we think we hear a voice in the spiritual realm, does it acknowledge that Jesus Christ came in the flesh? At times when I've asked that, I've received no answer but have gotten a weird, sometimes freaky sensation. Other times when I've asked it, the response has felt like a fatherly "Yes, it's me." Weird, yes, but we're talking about the supernatural here. Try it for yourself next time. What do you sense?

WAITING ON THE LORD

Outside of emergencies, God doesn't seem to send too many instant messages. Listening to God requires us to wait. As Psalm 130:5 says, "I wait for the LORD, my soul waits, and in his word I put my hope." Waiting like this demands time, a calm heart, and focused attention. In a fast-food, hyperactive culture, waiting is bad. We have microwaves and drive-throughs so we don't have to wait. But God is not subject to our culture; he relates to us more like a slow cooker. When we slow down and quiet our busy selves, we'll hear him.

The Spirit may also speak to us in a moment of rushing activity. But to hear him, we need ears that are trained to hear. That ability is developed through times of waiting on him. I've found that if my prayer time is rushed and I'm not listening, I can't expect to hear much from God either then or during the day. But when I condition myself to listen for what God may communicate, I'm more likely to perceive his voice even when I *am* in a rush.

DEVELOPING AN EAR TO HEAR

The ability to hear God does not come naturally to most of us. Similar to learning a new skill, a listening ear is cultivated. The Spirit of God communicates to us in different ways. Job 33:14 states, "God does speak—now one way, now another—though man may not perceive it." Since everyone is different, God communicates to us in different ways. For example, Kim receives words of knowledge and words of prophecy; I get mental impressions or gut feelings.

God never intends his communication to puff us up with spiritual pride or a controlling attitude toward others—rather it should keep us more submissive to him. Be careful when you say, "God told me . . ."—especially if it involves another person. If another person is involved in what God is telling you, he or she should hear from God too. When we test and hold such thoughts with humility, we will never manipulate others. We will only bless them.

PRAYER
~ Starter ~

Lord, teach me to quiet my heart and mind before you and listen. I want to be willing, patient, and perceptive. Above my own thoughts or thoughts from the world or from the devil, help me to discern your voice. . . .

LIFTED VOICE

I grew up in a church where people did not major in voice projection. The pastor prayed out loud; he was a professional. But most parishioners prayed silently—or maybe caught a quick nap. They spoke a mealtime blessing: "Come-Lord-Jesus-be-our-guest-may-these-gifts-to-us-be-blessed-Amen." At bedtime they recited, "Now-I-lay-me-down-to-sleep. . . ." Beyond that, the Lord's Prayer was one of the few that most nonpastors said out loud. Thankfully things have improved, yet vast numbers of Christians feel uncomfortable praying out loud and claim they don't know how.

But praying out loud is not complicated. It is simply verbalizing the prayer we already have in our minds.

VOICING PRAYER

Biblical figures talked to God out loud. David exclaimed in Psalm 142:1, "I cry aloud to the LORD; I lift up my voice to the LORD for mercy." In biblical times, praying out loud was so universally expected that when Hannah prayed silently in her heart yet moved her lips, Eli the priest thought she was drunk (1 Sam. 1:12–13).

Some people hesitate to voice their prayer because they're afraid it won't come out right. I once had church members who refused to pray out loud because they were intimidated by an older man who beseeched the Almighty in eloquent King James English. I finally convinced them that God also loves simple prayers from the heart, even if they have grammatical errors. Because I'd been an English major in college, I suspected that grammatical errors bothered me more than they bothered God.

Let's remember that when we talk to God, we're not addressing anyone else. The most others can legitimately do is agree or disagree with us. And if they disagree because of our imperfections, I suppose that gives them an opportunity to repent. At the end of a church service, Tony Campolo was "pumping hands," as he put it, when a woman said to him, "Reverend, you made three grammatical errors in your closing prayer." He replied, "I wasn't talking to you anyway, lady."[1]

Spoken prayers do not have to be sophisticated. Soon after we adopted our daughter, Irena, she began talking to God. She was three years old and couldn't speak any English. I was lying on the couch with a headache, and she walked over, laid her hands on me as she'd seen us do at church, and mumbled gibberish. Yet God knew her heart, and my headache was healed. At age six she was praying for her unsaved first grade classmates by name, especially if she got into fights with them.

Spoken prayer can range from loud to quiet. In the first loud prayer meeting I ever attended, I got mad at my soon-to-be wife. "Do these people think God needs a hearing aid?" I yelled. (Notice I *yelled*.) But I had come from the silent pray-ers' church and could not understand how people got so zealous when they connected with God. But because I was hungry for spiritual experiences, I subjected myself to the loud pray-ers. I gradually understood that when they shouted or cried loudly, it was not for God's sake but for their own. They were expressing their gut feelings. It was therapeutic and also helped them concentrate. But at other times these same people did pray in quiet voices.

SILENT PRAYER

Silent prayer is appropriate when meditating and listening to God, in formal settings, or to avoid attracting attention. And sometimes we just don't feel like talking. Yet it's unfortunate if we never speak up. How often have you caught your mind wandering when you pray silently? Thoughts can too easily float nebulously through our brains. Do you ever doze when you're praying? Silent prayer can actually sedate us as the peace of God settles in our hearts. If you're trying to sleep, that's great. But what if you prefer to be awake when you pray?

Medieval mystics gave lots of attention to disciplining their thoughts when they prayed silently. For them it was like a profession. But chances are that when you and I pray silently, our minds will wander more often and farther than when we pray out loud.

THREE REASONS TO VERBALIZE PRAYER

Verbalizing our prayer does three things. First, it forces us to clarify our thoughts. Rather than have vague, drifting notions, we speak out our thoughts. Speaking requires us to think coherently as we form combinations of words and ideas. Our prayer comes out with more meaning and clarity than it would if we merely entertained silent thoughts.

Second, as the sound of our own voice enters our ears, it stimulates us to pray more. Try it. In the dynamic of hearing and expressing, the aural stimulation increases our motivation to pray. We do not have to speak loudly. If we are the only ones who can hear our voices, that is enough.

Third, praying aloud rather than silently more fully expresses what's on our hearts. When we speak our prayer, the natural tendency is to be more passionate than when we're silent. Emotions flow more when they are expressed. Pouring our hearts out before God brings a psychological and emotional release. Though God is not concerned about how loudly we speak, he definitely calls us to pour our hearts out to him. Psalm 119:145 says, "I call with all my heart; answer me, O LORD."

PRAYING LOUDLY

Many people, including me, find it difficult to pray aloud when someone else is there. We feel self-conscious. Or maybe we're confessing something embarrassing. It seems that to verbally pour out our hearts, most of us have to be either alone or in a group of people who are also pouring out their hearts and can't hear what we're saying.

Kim and I used to irritate the neighbors when we prayed at night. Some thought we were mad at each other. Yes, we were having fights, but they were with the devil. We learned to shut the windows.

If you like praying loudly, take care that it doesn't become a false form of spirituality. Kim and I have dealt with too many people who had the idea that the louder they prayed, the more spiritual they were. When in a group they would always make sure to speak a little louder than everyone else, including the pastor. Time for a personal motive check! Praying out loud is not a show; it's a heart reaching to God.

RAISING VOICES TOGETHER

In prayer groups, non-Western, group-oriented cultures tend toward having everyone pray all at once, known as "simultaneous audible prayer." In Acts 4 Peter and John are released from prison and report back to the church. All together the people "raised their voices together in prayer to God" (v. 24). That's how simultaneous audible prayer works—everyone praying out loud at the same time. To the uninitiated it may sound disorderly, but it's really a harmony of people praying at the same time about the same thing. For many cultures this is natural.

Western, individualistic cultures tend toward having people take turns praying. It's considered respectful and orderly. This works fine, except that those who are not praying may risk drifting off into dreamland—especially if someone else prays long. If you pray with a group this way, I encourage you to voice affirmations of the one praying (the very word *amen* means to affirm or agree with what's been said). Or you could echo what the other person is saying—sort of praying quietly along the lines of that person's prayer. Doing this encourages the one praying, it builds up the group's dynamic, and it strengthens your and the group's agreement in faith. The people may have prayed this way in Acts 4:24 as well.

Both styles are learned, and both reach the ears of God. Whether you're in a group or alone, and whether you're praying loudly or quietly, remember that God is the only one you're talking to. And he loves the sound of your voice.

PRAYER
~ *Starter* ~

Lord, from the depth of my heart, I lift my voice to you. Hear me, O God. . . .

— DAY 13 —

SPECIFICALLY SPEAKING

On a dusty road outside Jericho sat a blind guy in his usual spot. Unable to get work, he spent his days begging for coins or morsels of food. He heard a commotion at the city gate. It sounded like a crowd. No one was yelling the way they did in protests or fights. It was orderly yet excited—like the crowds that surrounded important people. It came closer.

"Who is coming?" the blind guy asked.

No one paid attention to the beggar.

The throng came closer. The blind guy caught someone's garment. "Who is in the crowd?"

"Jesus of Nazareth." And the garment was yanked from his grip.

The blind guy had heard of Jesus. *The one called "Son of David." He has supernatural power. He heals.* "Jesus of Nazareth!" he shouted. "Have mercy on me!"

"Quiet, Bartimaeus," came a voice.

"Shut your mouth," another scolded.

Did Jesus say that? No. I've heard those voices before. "Jesus!" Louder this time. "Son of David, have mercy on me!"

"Will you shut up?" a voice snapped, followed by a curse.

"Son of David, have mercy on me!"

"Call him," came a voice, gentle yet in control.

The crowd quieted. Bartimaeus felt a hand tap his shoulder. "Cheer up! On your feet! He's calling you."

Bartimaeus threw aside his cloak, jumped to his feet, and stepped forward.

"What do you want me to do for you?" the gentle voice said.

What do I want him to do for me? Isn't it obvious? "Rabbi, I want to see."

"Go. Your faith has healed you."

The darkness of his eyes grew light. And he saw Jesus. (See Mark 10:46–52.)

Why did Jesus ask, "What do you want me to do for you?" Didn't he know? Of course he did. I think he wanted Bartimaeus to clearly identify what kind of mercy he sought rather than get by with vague, religious phrases. God responds to faith, and faith needs to be specific.

I suspect he wants us to clearly identify what we seek as well.

BEING VAGUE

When I harbor doubts about whether God will answer my prayer, my request becomes abstract, because that gives both

God and me an out. If a prayer goes unanswered, I'm off the hook and God is off the hook—because I don't expect anything anyway.

When I want nothing more than a generic blessing, my prayer is naturally generic. And I can make it sound spiritual. Anyone who's been around the church long enough can make themselves sound spiritual. But when I pray vaguely, I am answered vaguely. And that's being optimistic. If a prayer is not specific, how can anyone tell if it gets answered? In turn, if I can't tell whether I'm being answered, I'll tend to ask, "Why pray?"—and then lose interest in praying altogether.

Sometimes people are vague because it's painful to pray specifically and not be answered. This often happens when we pray for healing and don't receive it. What to do? I know it sounds like a mom saying, "Clean your room," but I'll say it: "Don't give up." That would be the advice of the widow in Luke 18:1–8. She didn't just ask for help; she specifically wanted justice against her adversary. She bugged the judge until she was answered. Jesus taught that parable to encourage us to never give up, and he wondered if we would have that kind of faith. He will allow us to go through the hardship of unanswered prayer, maybe to test us (like Job) or to grow our character (like Paul). He hopes that we won't give up.

Praying vaguely is like standing by a pool, afraid to swim, then going through the motions and pretending to swim. I finally figured out that even though I felt scared, I should plunge in. That way I *had* to swim or drown. And I swam. I prayed specifically whether things seemed important or not—healing of my back, exact amounts of money to pay bills. And I prayed just as specifically for other people's requests—students taking finals, people struggling with their businesses. Irena often had nightmares after my vague bedtime prayers. But whenever I prayed for good dreams and no nightmares, she slept well.

GETTING SPECIFIC

I hear people say, "The Lord worked in a special way." And I wonder, what kind of way? Or people say, "The Lord really blessed us." How? A true blessing is identifiable. Let's go beyond simply asking the Lord to "bless" people or meetings. Prayers of blessing in the Bible are specific and taken seriously—by God, by the ones who pray them, and by the ones who receive them. Biblical blessings address crops, health, relationships, social well-being, political freedom, and spiritual vitality. (And the curses are just as specific.) What particular blessing would you ask?

Being specific also works for confessing sin. We do not sin vaguely. We commit specific sins. So we need to confess them specifically. Specific forgiveness is light-years better than vague forgiveness. Vague forgiveness is as hard to identify as an answer to vague prayer.

When Jesus teaches on prayer in Luke 11:5–13, he gives an example of a friend who comes at midnight and asks for bread—not "some," but "three loaves" to be exact. Next he describes a son who asks for a fish, then an egg. He tells how ludicrous and malicious it would be for the father to give his son a snake instead of a fish or a scorpion instead of an egg. The specific request receives a specific, beneficial response—even when the request is unusual.

I was once part of a five-person crew on a forty-five-foot sailboat sailing from Hawaii to the Marshall Islands—two thousand miles across the middle of the Pacific. The first week we covered a thousand miles under sunny skies and strong wind. On the tenth day we entered the Intertropical Convergence Zone, also known as the Doldrums, where trade winds from the northern and southern hemispheres often converge and cancel each other out. The result for us was rain, rain, rain, and no wind. None. We sat in the rain for a day and used the motor, but we had to cut it to save our limited gas.

The next day, still sitting in that boat on a flat, endless ocean shrouded in perpetual rain, I wondered if God would be willing to blow on us. He did stuff like that in the Bible, didn't he? So I prayed for wind. The captain and his wife joined me, and the other two crew members scoffed. Within ten minutes wind began to blow. I'm not kidding. But it blew us in the wrong direction! So I asked God to turn the wind and blow us west. Within a half hour the wind shifted and blew us west. As we were thanking God and smiling at the scoffers, the wind increased and blew so hard we could barely manage the sails.

TRUSTING OUR FATHER

Sometimes we pray vaguely simply because we don't know what to pray—or we have too many interests to focus on just one. It's worth taking the time to think deeply about what you really wish to say to God. It doesn't matter if it sounds spiritual or not. What is your heart's deepest desire? If you are unsure, ask him.

You might say, "Lord, lead me how to pray." Andrew Murray writes that we should target our prayers:

> If in prayer we just pour out our hearts in a multitude of petitions, without taking time to see whether every petition is sent with the purpose and expectation of getting an answer, not many will reach the mark. But if, as in silence of soul we bow before the Lord, we were to ask such questions as these: What is now really my desire? Do I desire it in faith, expecting to receive? Am I now ready to place and leave it in the Father's bosom?[1]

God really does want to hear our specific desires—he's our loving Father. And he wants to see us trust him enough to put them into his hands and let them go—the same way any father would want his child to trust him. And if we simply do not know how to pray in a certain situation, we can trust him to do what is best.

Good fathers know when to be generous. Praying specifically does not limit God to what we ask. Sometimes he's like a dad who, when you ask him for a cheeseburger, buys you the mega meal deal. At one time more than half of those who attended our small church were teenagers. We had lots of life but not much money to pay the bills. I asked God about this, and he prompted me to pray for a $1,200 offering each Sunday. The next week, people gave just over $1,200, including a missionary love offering. The week after that we got blessed with a special donation of $7,500. For a while the offerings hovered around $1,200, as the Lord moved people who didn't even attend our church to give us their tithes and offerings. I wasn't going to pray for $1,000 because it was easier or $1,500 because I had macho faith. I asked the

Lord to show me the specific amount he wanted me to pray for. And because he knew what we needed, I completely stopped worrying about the needs. I knew I could trust him. I still do.

JUMP IN

If you don't know what to pray—and God doesn't seem to be leading you—the Bible can give direction. What does the Bible say about relationships, healing, financial provision, guidance, and comfort? (A Bible with a concordance in the back is good for finding verses.) Specific prayer can test and increase your trust in God's Word. We'll look at that in day 14.

Remember how vague versus specific prayer is like standing beside a pool and pretending to swim versus jumping in? If you haven't already, I encourage you to jump in with me. Identify what you're praying for. Then actually expect it. Name the need or a promise in the Bible.

Remember Jesus' question to Bartimaeus. Faith puts itself on the line. Faith is specific.

PRAYER
~ *Starter* ~

> Lord, guide me in how I should pray. . . . (Wait quietly for God's leading. Or pray according to a promise in Scripture or for something on your own list. Expect.)

— *DAY 14* —

PRAYING GOD'S WORD

On March 27, 1977, a bomb scare at Las Palmas in the Canary Islands rerouted all flights from there to a small airport on the island of Tenerife. Eighteen 747s crowded the taxiway for four hours. Hoping to minimize time wasted, the pilots of a KLM 747 fueled up. They finally received clearance and jetted down the runway for takeoff in dense fog. There was no ground radar to warn them of a Pan Am 747 crossing the runway.

Burdened with 144,000 pounds of fuel, the KLM couldn't gain enough lift, and its landing gear ripped through the top of the Pan Am's fuselage. The KLM collapsed upon the Pan Am and unleashed a flood of jet fuel. Flames engulfed both planes. It was the worst airline disaster in history.

Out of the horror, one passenger's story stands out. Norman Williams was a man who read his Bible. As flames engulfed him he remembered Isaiah 43:2, where God promises, "When you walk through the fire, you will not be burned; the flames will not set you ablaze." He began quoting the verse and yelling over and over, "Lord, I stand upon your Word. I stand upon your Word."

At fifty-two years of age and 250 pounds, Williams found himself inexplicably able to climb (or leap or be lifted—he doesn't remember) through a hole above. He jumped onto the wing, then to the ground, where he shattered his left foot. He quipped that he hadn't quoted any verses on not getting broken bones. But he had no burns. Out of 687 people on board the two planes, 70 survived, and most of them had severe burns and emotional trauma, requiring ongoing medical and psychological treatment. Every other person in Williams's section of the plane was burned beyond identification. Except for his foot and cut fingers, Williams was fine.[1] "Circumstances meant nothing," he testified later.

All through the Bible we read about God fulfilling promises and doing amazing miracles. And we read of the needs and prayers of his people. We have similar needs. Does God care for us as much as he did them? I think he does. Then can't we believe him for specific, sometimes miraculous, answers that he has promised in his Word? Norman Williams would tell us yes.

THE EARLY CHURCH PRAYED SCRIPTURE

In Acts 4:23–31 when the Jewish ruling council released Peter and John from their arrest, the two reported back to the

Jerusalem church. Immediately all the people gathered there joined together in a loud group prayer. They started by giving glory to God. Then they prayed Scripture by quoting Psalm 2:1–2. After this they presented to God the problem of the political opposition they faced, and they offered themselves to be part of God's answer. They did not pray for their own protection, only for power to witness and do miracles. God shook the place, apparently with an earthquake, and filled them with the Holy Spirit.

Praying Scripture for the early church meant that they related a Bible verse to their personal situation. In their case Psalm 2:1–2 spoke prophetically of earthly rulers who stood against God and particularly against the Messiah—just as the Jewish leaders now stood against them and their proclamation of Jesus the Messiah.

In the same way, we can apply a Bible verse to whatever we face, just as Norman Williams did. Even if the outcome is not miraculous, God's Word still gives us comfort, hope, and courage to face our challenge.

WHEN WE PRAY SCRIPTURE

When I pray for senior citizens who are believers, I quote Psalm 92:12, 14: "The righteous will flourish like a palm tree. . . . They will still bear fruit in old age, they will stay fresh and green." For healing of an illness, I remember Psalm 103:3, which says the Lord "heals all your diseases." In tragedy or misfortune, I recall Romans 8:28, which promises, "In all things God works for the good of those who love him, who have been called according to his purpose." Praying according to biblical promises guides my prayer and increases my faith for an answer. It's as though I'm praying along with God rather than on my own.

God knows what his Word says; he doesn't need us to tell him. So although we give glory to God by praising him with what's written, we pray his Word mainly for our sakes. Internalizing what the Bible says builds our confidence when we pray, because we're praying not merely by our own desires but according to his promises.

Jeanne Guyon was a gutsy lady who lived in France at the turn of the eighteenth century and taught on prayer and intimacy with God. Her teaching that any serious Christian could be close to God delighted the common people. But it threatened Roman Catholic church leaders, and they imprisoned her for years. (It sometimes amazes me that Christianity survived the church.) We can still benefit from the teachings for which she suffered. She was one of the first people to articulate praying Scripture:

> You do not read quickly; you read very slowly. You do not move from one passage to another, not until you have *sensed* the very heart of what you have read. You may want to take that portion of Scripture that has touched you and turn it into prayer. . . .
>
> "Praying the Scripture" is not judged by *how much* you read but by the *way* you read. If you read quickly, it will benefit you little. You will be like a bee that merely skims the surface of a flower. Instead, in this new way of reading with prayer, you become as the bee who penetrates into the *depths* of the flower.[2]

Guyon's approach goes beyond understanding what God's Word means to grasping its intention. If we grab a handy Bible verse and use it to get what we want, we may be playing games rather than praying Scripture. But when we let a verse penetrate our thinking and apply it to our situation, then address it back to God, that's praying Scripture. We're thinking God's thoughts after him, praying according to his will as recorded for the ages.

When we pray Scripture, we actually hold God to his Word. That's a scary thought. Who are we to hold the almighty God to his Word? This is who: his children. John 1:12 says that to all who receive and believe him, he gives "the right to become children of God." Hebrews 4:16 tells us we can "approach the throne of grace with confidence." Yet few of us experience the fullness of God's promises. It may be partly because not many hold God to his Word enough to ask and trust. He answers and blesses those of us who believe God's Word and claim it in our prayers.

WAYS TO PRAY SCRIPTURE

We can pray Scripture in at least three ways. I'll use 2 Corinthians 1:3–4 as an example.

Read it verbatim. Begin with, "Lord, your Word says . . ." Then read the text back to God, affirming what it says: "Lord, your Word says you are 'the Father of compassion and the God of all comfort, who comforts us in all our troubles, so that we can comfort those in any trouble with the comfort we ourselves have received from God.' Lead me to experience this, O God."

Personalize it. Change the Bible verse to first person singular (i.e., "I," "me," "my"). Then read it as an affirmation of faith in what God has said in his Word, as if it were written to you personally: "Lord, according to your Word, you comfort me in all my troubles, so that I can comfort those in any trouble with the comfort I myself have received from you."

Paraphrase it. Whether you're reading or quoting from memory, paraphrase what the verse says in the context of what you're praying about: "Lord, you are the God of all comfort. You comfort me when I have trouble, and you know my trouble today. Thank you that I can take the comfort I receive from you and comfort others with it."

Try all three. You will find that praying Scripture brings a richness and depth to your prayer that can be found in no other way.

SCRIPTURE TO PRAY

Here are some Bible passages that cover a variety of topics and lend themselves well to prayer. Half come from Psalms and half from the New Testament.

Psalms		New Testament	
1:1–3	the one whom God blesses	Mark 11:22–26	mountain-moving faith
23	the Lord is my shepherd	John 8:31–36	the truth will set you free
34	God's redeeming presence	John 16:33	Christ has overcome the world
42	sadness and longing for God	Acts 2:42–47	fellowship of believers
46	God, our refuge and strength	Romans 8:28–32	God works for good

Psalms		New Testament	
51:10–17	repentance	*Romans 12:1–2*	a living sacrifice
63	hunger for God	*1 Corinthians 10:13*	God's help in temptation
73:21–26	bitterness turns to hope	*1 Corinthians 15:57–58*	our victory in Christ
77	remember what God has done	*2 Corinthians 1:3–11*	comfort and deliverance
84:1–2, 10	desire for God's presence	*2 Corinthians 9:6–11*	sow and reap generously
91	God's protection	*Galatians 2:20*	crucified with Christ
92:12–15	freshness in old age	*Ephesians 6:10–18*	stand with armor of God
100	wholehearted worship of God	*Philippians 4:4–9*	rejoice, God's peace
103	God is everything to us	*Colossians 3:12–17*	Christian character
112	blessed is the one who fears God	*1 Thessalonians 5:16–18*	rejoice, pray, give thanks
119:67–75	the value of affliction	*1 Peter 2:9–10*	we are a royal priesthood
139	God knows and sees all	*1 John 2:15–17*	do not love the world
146	God lifts up those in need	*Revelation 4–5*	the throne room of God

There is nothing in all of life that is not addressed in one way or another by a principle found in Scripture. As you read your Bible, take note of passages that particularly speak to your situation and things you pray for. Trust God for what he says in his Word, and see what he does in turn.

PRAYER
~ *Starter* ~

Lord, your Word says . . . I believe your Word
and trust that you will do in my life what you
promise here. . . .

— *DAY 15* —

THE EMPTY-STOMACH
EFFECT

Jerry Falwell, the then chancellor of Liberty University and pastor of the 22,000-member Thomas Road Baptist Church in Lynchburg, Virginia, was in trouble. Disastrous trouble. His university faced seventy million dollars in debt and loss of its accreditation. In response to that, he went on a forty-day fast, drinking only water and juices. Twenty-five days after the fast was over, he did another forty-day fast. Aside from his losing eighty-two pounds, by the end of his second fast the school had received over fifty million dollars in donations, and the crisis was overcome. On top of this, he reported that fasting among people in Lynchburg led to spiritual awakening, saying, "This is not the same university. This is not the same church. I am not the same man."[1]

Fasting is a physical way of humbling ourselves before God. Fasting says to God, "I'm serious about this!" Because it carries humble, earnest prayer into the tangible, physical realm, it brings about a brokenness before God that can come in no other way. That is why fasting is often a key factor of spiritual breakthrough such as answered prayer or a powerful sense of God's presence.

BROADLY SPEAKING

Broadly speaking, fasting can be seen as the voluntary denial of any normal function for the sake of intensified spiritual activity. This means we can fast from anything: food, activities, or entertainment. The point is that it's a sacrificial focus on God, where we would have otherwise indulged ourselves or given our attention to something else.

Except for special days in the Old Testament, the Bible gives no commands or rules about fasting. It's strictly voluntary and nothing to get legalistic about. Yet examples throughout the Bible suggest that God highly encourages it. And Jesus did say, "*When* you fast . . ." (Matt. 6:16, emphasis added). Fasting is a good practice that fosters self-discipline, humility, and focused prayer. Since we have freedom and flexibility in how we fast, I suggest that we be like God and give ourselves lots of grace.

STRICTLY SPEAKING

Strictly speaking, fasting is refraining from eating, not to lose weight (though that may be a bonus byproduct) but to intensify our seeking of God. Three general types of fasting are practiced.

In a dry fast, a person does not eat or drink anything at all. When Moses went to the top of Mount Sinai, he stayed there for forty days, undergoing a dry fast (Deut. 9:18). Jesus underwent a dry fast for forty days in the desert (Matt. 4:2). First Kings 19:8 implies that Elisha's forty-day fast may have been dry. A forty-day dry fast is obviously supernatural, for under normal circumstances no human can go without water for that long. The king of Nineveh proclaimed over the whole city a brief dry fast for urgent repentance, and God spared the city (Jonah 3:5–10). Esther requested a dry fast of the Jews in Susa for three days before she made her request to King Xerxes (Esther 4:16). But because our bodies need water, I'd recommend one of the next two kinds of fasting.

In a total fast, a person does not eat anything but does drink liquids. Much of the fasting in the Bible was probably done this way. Scripture always indicates when a fast was dry. But in most cases Scripture does not say whether people drank or not, and it is commonly understood that in the majority, if not all, of these cases, they drank liquids. This is the kind of fast most commonly done today as well. Most people drink water or fruit juice.

In a partial fast, a person abstains from certain types of food, particularly meat, nonessentials, or fine foods. Sometimes people call this a "Daniel fast," because Daniel "mourned for three weeks" and "ate no choice food; no meat or wine touched [his] lips; and [he] used no lotions at all until the three weeks were over" (Dan. 10:2–3). Choice foods would include any kind of fancy dining, snacks, condiments, sweets, or desserts. Partial fasting sticks with the basics of simple, vegetarian food—and the basics of grooming as well.

God honors all types of fasting. His leading and our physical capacity may determine which one we do at any given time.

WHY FAST?

Fasting in the Bible is done for several reasons:

- Repentance and humbling before God
  (Nehemiah 1; Daniel 9; Jonah 3:5–9)
- Mourning over death
  (1 Sam. 31:13; 2 Sam. 1:11–12; 3:31–35)
- Petition
  —for breakthrough in times of distress
    (2 Chron. 20:1–4; Esther 4:14–16)
  —for healing (2 Sam. 12:15–17)
  —for guidance or understanding (Acts 13:1–3)
  —for protection (Ezra 8:21–23)
  —when beginning a new ministry (Matt. 4:1–2)

Fasting has been widely practiced throughout church history. In the early church, new believers fasted before they were baptized, and the church practiced regular fasts. After the Roman Empire legalized Christianity, believers no longer faced the rigors of persecution. Fearing they would grow lax, many disciplined themselves by fasting, especially the groups of monks who went to live in the desert. For most great Christian leaders through the centuries, fasting has been central to their lives and ministries. Writing in the fifth century, Peter Chrysologus captured the essence of what Isaiah says in chapter 58 about how fasting relates to social justice: "Fasting is the soul of prayer, and helping the needy is the life-blood of fasting."[2]

Today most people tend to fast when they ask God for answers to prayer or for help in times of distress. Some also fast as a form of spiritual discipline, as people did in the early church. In any case, the hunger pangs or cravings for certain foods continuously remind people to pray and find consolation in God.

How Long?

Though Moses and Jesus fasted for forty days, Daniel did his partial fast for three weeks. Fasting in the Bible was commonly done for a day. The only regularly required fast in Scripture was for the Day of Atonement, which lasted twenty-four hours (Lev. 16:29–34). Other fasts were done from sunup to sundown. Sometimes biblical figures fasted for several days or until a goal was reached or a prayer was answered. Similarly, we can fast regularly or when desired; we can fast one meal, a whole day, several days, or even weeks. We've got freedom here. Think about it, ask God about it, and try what's best for you.

From a practical standpoint, if you are concerned about nourishment, take vitamins and drink natural fruit or vegetable juices.

If you have health problems or any other concerns, consult a physician before fasting. For those of us who live in wealthy nations, we are so used to three meals a day that many of us don't realize how well the body can cope, even benefit, from fasting. Periodic fasting cleanses the body by allowing cells to discharge built-up chemicals, metals, and toxins. It also gives our liver a needed break.[3]

ATTITUDES AND BENEFITS OF FASTING

To many Christians, fasting is not an appealing discipline. But one of its hidden virtues is that it stands against all-too-prevalent habits of self-indulgence. The simple act of refraining from food, or anything else, helps us grow in the maturity of rising above the incessant tendency to satisfy every perceived need. Fasting is therapeutic for the soul.

Jesus reminds us not to make a show of our fasting. He tells us to groom and behave normally, that God is the only one who needs to know we're fasting, and that he will reward us (Matt. 6:16–18).

Isaiah challenges us to take fasting beyond personal concerns and into the realm of social welfare and justice. He says the Lord would have us bring justice and freedom to the oppressed, and feed, clothe, and shelter the poor (Isa. 58:6–14). Donating money otherwise spent on food is one common practice. What else might you do?

Intimacy with God and frequent breakthroughs in prayer seem particularly common to those who fast. I know many people who have experienced answered prayer after fasting, and some would never consider going long without fasting. I generally fast on Fridays, and I can say that after years of doing it, then not doing it, then doing it again, I live closer to God and see more answered prayer when I fast than when I don't.

The discipline of fasting is both physically and spiritually rewarding, but ultimately it cannot be adequately explained. It has to be experienced. If God leads you to try it, you will soon discover its benefits. Yet it needs more than a quickie onetime try, where you give up if you don't feel anything. Give it the chance of several experiences over a period of time. I suspect you'll gain a desire to fast more.

I encourage you to remember three things: Fasting enhances the seriousness of your prayer by taking it to the physical level. Start where you're at and go from there. God knows your heart and body; let him lead you.

PRAYER
~ Starter ~

Lord, I fast as a sign of humility and brokenness before you. I offer my body as a living expression of my prayer. I'm serious about seeking you today. Lead me deep into your heart. . . .

EXTERNAL
HELPS

— *DAY 16* —

ROOM RESERVATIONS

For years Kim and I lived in apartments where we had no extra space to set apart for prayer. God didn't need a designated location to talk with me; he heard me wherever I was. But I, the human, craved a physical place set aside for prayer. Without one, I got distracted and tended not to pray much. When I did pray, I had a hard time focusing. To overcome my weakness, I needed a special spot where I could agree with myself that when I was there, the only thing I did was pray and read the Bible.

No holy site was nearby, no yard, park, or seaside—just streets and freeways. So in a corner of our apartment, I laid out a little rug and a small, low table. That rug became my sacred space. The only thing I allowed myself, or anyone else, to do on that rug was to pray and read the Bible. Holding to this pattern meant that every time I sat there, I automatically focused on God. If I needed to use the space for other things, I folded up the rug until the next day.

THE IMPORTANCE OF A PLACE OF PRAYER

A consistent, focused prayer life thrives on an established, regular place. The physical surroundings of a setting devoted to prayer tell our brains, "Focus on God." Without such a place, everywhere we pray will be just another location for doing things in a busy day.

We don't know all the details of biblical leaders, but most of them weren't settled in one place like most of us. Biblical references to places of prayer frequently mention the tabernacle that the Israelites hauled around the desert or the temple they built in Jerusalem. Many Old Testament figures built an altar in a field or on a mountain, where they worshiped and sacrificed. In the New Testament, besides in the temple, people prayed in synagogues.

None of us lives around the corner from the tabernacle or the temple (they no longer exist), but church sanctuaries are usually not too far away. These are great places to pray during the weekdays—and the Roman Catholic ones are always open. Built into the architecture of any sanctuary, whether simple or ornate, is a concentration on God—the design practically focuses on God for you. I highly recommend sanctuaries.

If you don't have a church sanctuary nearby, you can lay claim to almost anywhere. Designate a special space that would otherwise be just an ordinary locale but to you is set aside as a rendezvous point with God. The prophet Daniel did this. Daniel 6:10 tells us he "went home to his upstairs room where the windows opened toward Jerusalem. Three times a day he got down on his knees and prayed." This guy went to the same room three times a day. And besides that, he opened the windows facing Jerusalem to give him more inspiration and focus. He was so consistent in this that his enemies knew exactly when and where to find him praying.

Jesus was homeless—let's call it "itinerant"—and since he was always on the move, he had no consistent place to pray. So he found a consistent *type* of place. In Mark 1:35 we find that "very early in the morning, while it was still dark, Jesus got up, left the house and went off to a solitary place, where he prayed." For Jesus to connect with his Father, he consistently found secluded areas.

Four times the Gospel of Luke tells about Jesus' habit of finding solitary settings in which to pray: "At daybreak Jesus went out to a solitary place" (4:42). "Jesus often withdrew to lonely places and prayed" (5:16). "Jesus went out to a mountainside to pray" (6:12). "Jesus went out as usual to the Mount of Olives" (22:39). He regularly looked for solitary locations to pray. And in bustling Jerusalem, he headed for the Mount of Olives, to his favorite grove of olive trees—the Garden of Gethsemane.

Jesus didn't do this only for himself. His disciples were getting worn out from ministering to endless streams of people, so at one point Jesus took them by boat to a solitary place for a group getaway (Mark 6:30–32). But then five thousand men plus women and children showed up. After Jesus fed them all, he put the disciples in a boat and dismissed the crowd. Then he "went up on a mountainside to pray" (v. 46). Jesus probably could have drawn a map of the quiet places in Israel.

What would be your quiet places?

ESTABLISHING A PRAYER PLACE

Susanna Wesley, John Wesley's mother, had lots of kids tearing around—ten of them (nine others did not survive infancy). She had nowhere to escape for prayer. So she got creative and established a space right in the middle of the kids. It is said that she sat in her rocking chair and put her apron over her head, which was a sign to her army of children that Mommy was talking to God, so don't bother her.

Charles Simeon, who taught at Cambridge University in the early 1800s, maintained a vibrant—and amusing—prayer life in the midst of a busy schedule. Along the rooftop of his living quarters stretched a fenced walkway, where he would walk back and forth, praying. To the people below who saw him each day, the rooftop path became known as "Simeon's Walk." And no, he never fell off the roof.

So if you don't have a church sanctuary, a Sahara desert solitude, or a Mount Everest view—no worries. Any location can become set apart—sacred to you—if you designate it that way. I know a guy whose prayer place was on top of a boulder in his backyard. Another parked his car under a tree at the far corner of a parking lot before work. Just devote the location you choose to spending time with God.

Which of these ideas could work for you to establish a special place to pray?

- A room or space somewhere in your home
- An empty room at school or work during lunch hour
- The front seat of your car parked in a quiet, shady spot
- A park bench or picnic table
- A spot in the backyard
- _____

I've found it important to have enough light to read the Bible. I also make sure it's quiet and peaceful enough to think and meditate. And the more solitary the better. At times we're all glad for a place where we can freely express ourselves and not worry about what other people think. Like those days when we can't contain our joy or anger or sorrow, and we pour ourselves out before God—the way Job and David did.

If you travel a lot, you'll have to improvise as Jesus did. I recommend designating a corner of your hotel room—and double your effectiveness by covering the TV with a towel. That may sound silly, but a towel over the TV, even if the TV is in a cabinet, can go a long way in reducing its power of distraction. Try that at home too.

In a worst-case scenario, if you simply cannot find or make a designated physical space to pray, take a tip from Jewish practice and wear something. Really. When reading the Torah and praying in the synagogue, Jews put on a prayer shawl (*tallit*) that covers the head and shoulders. Along with the rich symbolism it provides, the prayer shawl helps them focus their prayers just

as a special place would. So if it works for you, wear something
that by its dedicated use will tell your brain, "Focus on the Lord!"

BREAKING THE ROUTINE

Having said all that about the importance of a consistent place
for prayer, sometimes it may help to break the routine. Occasionally praying somewhere different can keep you from falling into a
rut of overfamiliarity with your surroundings. If you find yourself
bored or lulled to complacency and suspect your location has
anything to do with it, temporarily pray somewhere else. Just
as a regular place is important for consistency, an occasional
change can be stimulating. When managed well, change can
be consistency's best friend.

PRAYER
~ *Starter* ~

Lord, though you reign over all the world, I
dedicate this place as sacred to my time with
you. In this place help me focus myself on
you. . . .

— DAY *17* —

SPECIAL APPOINTMENTS

Sixteenth- and seventeenth-century Puritans practiced a spirituality far different from that voiced from Roman Catholic cloisters and most Protestant pulpits. Puritans developed their spirituality within common family life, amid the daily routines of work and home. To do this, they had to designate time within those demands—just as we do today. In addition to Sunday worship, both family and private prayer were expected of a good Puritan. Author Allen Carden discovered that "manuals with appropriate prayers were published and were apparently followed quite closely by Puritan families. Morning prayers emphasized confession of sin, a request for forgiveness, and thanksgiving to God for his beneficence. . . . Prayers in the evening before retiring often focused on the analogy of laying down in death and awakening to new life, with requests made for safety throughout the night."[1] Only in the late nineteenth century did the term *Puritan* get falsely associated with joyless, repressive legalism. Though strict, the Puritans' practice of Christianity was biblical, spiritual, and generally healthy.

The poet Anne Bradstreet sailed to the New World in 1630, ten years after the first Pilgrims. She endured all the burdens of a wife and mother in those hard years of Puritan settlement. Yet in the midst of the sweat, she maintained a profound spirituality. Her prayer life and deep journey toward union with God, as evidenced in her poetry,[2] bear striking resemblances to Teresa of Avila, except that Teresa was a nun.

We can thank the Puritans for leaving us the legacy of developing spiritual life in the midst of daily routines. Perhaps the most important thing we learn from them is to establish a regular prayer time.

ESTABLISH A PRAYER TIME

Of course we can pray at any time of the day. Yet a consistent, healthy spiritual life usually needs a daily "God time." The consistency of what we do at a certain hour ingrains itself in our brains. Without such a time, prayer can easily get pushed aside in a busy day—and even in a not-so-busy day. At best, our prayer lives will lack the boundaries essential to focused, unrushed periods set aside to connect with God.

Most people don't have a problem with spending too much time in prayer. Some of us have minds hardwired to do all the things on our chock-full to-do lists, which can mean that spending time just sitting around reading the Bible and praying for more than five minutes feels like a waste of time. That's what I used to think. My life was stressed out. But I learned that time spent with my heavenly Father actually reduced my stress—and helped me prioritize everything in my life so that I had less on my list. Richard Foster similarly says, "We willingly 'waste our time' in this manner as a lavish love offering to the Father. God will then take what looks like a foolish waste and use it to bring us further into his loving presence."[3]

DO IT IN THE MORNING

As we saw previously, Mark 1:35 says that "very early in the morning, while it was still dark, Jesus got up, left the house and went off to a solitary place, where he prayed." Why so early? The next two verses tell us: "Simon and his companions went to look for him, and when they found him, they exclaimed: 'Everyone is looking for you!'" (vv. 36–37). Jesus hardly ever got any peace! He had to pray early.

King David, a guy who was busy running the country, says in Psalm 5:3, "In the morning, O LORD, you hear my voice; in the morning I lay my requests before you and wait in expectation." Time with God is ideally the first thing to do when you get up in the morning and are awake enough to do anything. If you need caffeine or a shower to wake up, just be careful to minimize what you do before you pray so you don't distract yourself from it.

The irony is that the more demanding your daily schedule, the more necessary it is to set aside time for prayer. God's blessing and guidance will make a huge difference as the day wears on. John Wesley, the great eighteenth-century evangelist and church leader, understood that. He rose at 4:00 every morning to pray. He would devote every minute of the day to ministry and often worked until 10 p.m.[4] His ministry changed the world. You may not change the world, but you get the idea that morning prayer will benefit the whole day.

If I don't maintain a morning rendezvous with God, someone or something else will invariably come along, and time with God will become another lost wish. This is where waking up on time is a spiritual act, because the rest of the day charges in before midmorning.

If you're like me, you might want to stay up late and finish one more thing. If you're not like me, God bless you. I'll tell you what I tell myself: sometimes the most spiritual thing you can do is to go to bed on time.

WHAT IF MORNINGS JUST DON'T WORK?

"Gotta get to school." "Gotta get to work." "Gotta get the kids to school—yikes, I'm late for work." Often morning rush hour doesn't start on the freeway—it starts inside the house. If that's true for you no matter what you try, find a consistent morning break time. If that's not possible, you've got lunch time. Many people with company lunch breaks take no more than half their break to eat. The rest of the time they talk, exercise, or read a book.

That's fine, but if that's your earliest free time of the day, Jesus would love to spend it with you—even more than your colleagues would. He also has the world's bestselling book for you to read.

If nothing else, pray in the morning and read the Bible during lunch break. Be creative. We all have our own home, school, commuting, or work situations. And God is always ready to receive our welcome.

Occasionally people pray for extended periods late at night, which is wonderful. And most of us say a prayer before we sleep. But a regular time with God is most beneficial early in the day. That way we can reap the maximum benefits throughout our waking hours.

A BOUNDARY OF TIME

Have you ever made the mistake of trying to maintain a good relationship with someone where your moments together were always bullied by time pressures, people pressures, and things-to-do pressures? It didn't go very well, did it? In the same way, prayer is spending guarded time with one who wants a good relationship.

I've found it helpful to establish a minimum length for my God time. That may sound legalistic, but a set period of time safeguards our freedom in prayer. Without one, endless demands will intrude and distract. We do ourselves a favor by guaranteeing the gift of a certain amount of unpressured, uncluttered time with God—just as we would ensure ourselves enough time with someone we love.

If you are not used to praying, start with five or ten minutes, even if it feels superficial at first. You may enjoy it and eventually go longer. Some people set apart as much as one or two hours a day, and a few go for three. I've never known God to complain about people spending too much time with him.

As soon as you do this, you can be sure that everything imaginable will try to invade your God time. Most of it will be legitimate things that need your attention—later. The phone will ring. You'll remember that errand to do. Projects with deadlines will stare at you. Laundry will wail, "Wash me!" Messes will moan, "Organize me!" What to do?

Practice intentional neglect. For the duration of the time you pray, intentionally neglect all the other things shouting for your attention: dirty dishes, scattered toys, phone calls, emails, bills, letters, and homework. They *will* get done—*afterward* (except maybe for screaming babies). Plan your time with God like you would with someone you respect. If that incoming phone call is important, the person will leave a message. By intentionally neglecting everything that cries for your attention, you will find that your time with God is more peaceful, focused, and fulfilling. And you'll find that you are freer to speak to and hear from your Maker.

Keep the Routine

Although changing a prayer place can avoid monotony and bring stimulus, I have never found the same benefit in changing a prayer time. It seems to be something we should try to keep sacred every day, wherever we are. We can always pray at any time. But that special daily appointment with the one who loves us infuses his life-giving presence into any good, bad, or busy day.

PRAYER
~ *Starter* ~

Lord, increase in my heart the value of spending time with you so that I will always prioritize you in my daily schedule. I look forward to it and will guard it. . . .

— DAY *18* —

LIFTED HANDS AND FEET

I once prayed with another guy on weekday afternoons. You could call it "afternoons with a zombie." I was the zombie, and my biggest problem was staying awake. Especially when we quietly waited on the Lord. And always on hot summer days. I felt as if my head were stuffed with cotton and my eyelids weighed five pounds each. So I prayed loudly, and when my friend was praying, I agreed in prayer. Yet I still nodded off. Then I'd jerk my head up, embarrassed. So I lifted my hands and rocked my body. I stood up. I walked. When my friend wasn't looking, I slapped my cheeks. Finally I stayed awake. As long as I kept moving, I was okay. But the minute I stopped, my body lapsed back into the afternoon blahs, and my mind drifted with it.

Bodies and minds work together. What do you observe when a child is earnestly asking a parent for something (besides his or her moaning)? Look at the little person: feet jumping; arms flapping; body swaying, collapsing on the ground, and then popping up again.

As time passed, I learned that part of the cure for zombie prayers was through movement—my body expressing my prayer.

LIFTED HANDS AND EYES

The apostle Paul instructs believers to "lift up holy hands in prayer" (1 Tim. 2:8). This means that when we pray, we lift our hands upward. Over and over that is how the Bible tells us to pray.

Most Christians abide by what I call the "Sunday school position for prayer": eyes closed, head bowed, hands clasped together. On every count this is exactly the opposite of what Scripture says. My theory is that somewhere in the misty past, this was the only way the Sunday school teacher got Johnny to stop pinching Sally and the other kids to stop passing notes and giggling long enough for that teacher to pray. Perhaps these kids grew up and figured they should always pray that way, because that's how they did it in Sunday school. For whatever traditional or cultural reasons, too many of us pray in stiff, closed postures.

God gives us another pattern. Throughout the Bible, the lifting of hands is synonymous with praise and prayer. When the Israelites battled the Amalekites in the desert at Rephidim

(Exod. 17:10–13), Moses went to the top of a hill to intercede for his army. The text doesn't even say he prayed. It says he "held up his hands" (v. 11). As long as his hands were upheld (in the position of prayer), the Israelites were winning. When he got tired and lowered his hands (breaking from prayer), the Israelites began losing. So Aaron and Hur sat him down, stood to his right and left, and held up his hands until the Israelites won.

Solomon modeled this pattern of uplifted hands when he dedicated the temple: "He stood on the platform and then knelt down"—body language for respect and humility. Then he "spread out his hands toward heaven" and prayed (2 Chron. 6:13).

Psalms repeatedly shows the lifting of hands as the posture of prayer: "I call to you for help, as I lift up my hands toward your Most Holy Place" (28:2). "I will praise you as long as I live, and in your name I will lift up my hands" (63:4). "I call to you, O LORD, every day; I spread out my hands to you" (88:9). "I spread out my hands to you; my soul thirsts for you like a parched land" (143:6). The people of Israel didn't just pray with their mouths; they got their bodies into it.

As for the eyes? "I lift my eyes to the hills—where does my help come from?" (Ps. 121:1). "I lift up my eyes to you, to you whose throne is in heaven" (Ps. 123:1). "Lift your eyes and look to the heavens" (Isa. 40:26). "Lift up your eyes to the heavens" (Isa. 51:6). In John 17:1 Jesus "looked toward heaven and prayed." So it's okay for you to open your eyes and look to heaven when you pray. That works great outside or in an awe-inspiring cathedral, but if opening your eyes causes a distraction because you spot a cobweb on the ceiling, go ahead and shut those eyes.

As for your head, you can't bow it when you're lifting your eyes. Try it—you can't. Raising our heads is implicit in all the verses on lifting the eyes. In Scripture, heads are bowed for one of two reasons. One is a sign of humility. In Psalms we read, "In reverence will I bow down" (5:7) and "Come, let us bow down in worship" (95:6). This bowing is often accompanied by the whole-body posture of being flat on the face. It is related to the Greek word for worship, *proskuneo*, which means "to kiss the hem," and it was first used to describe a king or general lying prostrate and kissing the garment hem of the one who had conquered him.

Second, people bow when the glory of God is so strong in a place that there's little to do but bow to the ground in worship. This occurred at the dedication of the temple in 2 Chronicles 7:1–3: "Fire came down from heaven and consumed the burnt offering and the sacrifices, and the glory of the LORD filled the temple" such that the priests could not even enter. The Israelites outside watching this "knelt on the pavement with their faces to the ground." Minus the fire and smoke, God's presence in times of worship or prayer can still be strong. Many times I have been among people who spontaneously knelt, and often wept, as they sensed the presence of God come over the assembly. Blessed are you when you have this experience.

BODY LANGUAGE

What difference does our prayer posture make? It's in the body language. Try the simplest experiment: Stand in front of a friend (or an enemy) with your arms crossed. Then open your arms as if ready to embrace. Ask that person if your two body postures expressed any meaning to them. Then see if you felt different with each posture.

When we bow our heads and clasp our hands, the posture tends to draw us inward. When we lift our heads and raise our hands to heaven, the posture releases us outward and upward. We become more open to God, even more aware of his presence, when we express ourselves physically. An outstretched hand is also a physical sign of surrender. An open palm expresses openness, a heart seeking God.

Besides lifting your hands, try clapping them. The Bible tells us to do that too in Psalm 47:1. Clapping shows appreciation and joy. It also stimulates prayer, both by its wake-up sound and through body movement.

LIFTED FEET

When I first prayed with people who walked around while praying, I thought they were like androids pacing in circles. Weirdos. Then I started doing it. And I realized the simple reason why: the movement keeps me alert. Now I often walk when I pray, whether back and forth or in laps around the sanctuary or my backyard.

Like many writers, Ernest Hemingway often paced the room when he wrote. His mind was clearer and sharper when his body moved. Sometimes he put his typewriter on top of a dresser so he could type standing up. His Nobel Prize would suggest that his method worked. I researched why.

Our brains use roughly 20 percent of our body's oxygen. The exact amount the brain uses relates directly to the amount of its activity.[1] The more active the brain becomes, the more blood it requires. Conversely, the more blood that is pumped into our gray matter, the more ability the brain has for mental activity and alertness. So when we move around, our blood flow increases and our brains become more alert. In addition to this, physical movement causes more oxygenated blood to flow to muscles, which stimulates the entire body.

Physical activity also causes the pituitary gland to release endorphins, hormones relating to mood, alertness, and pain relief. The brain contains hundreds of billions of nerve cells. Between them are contact points called synapses. Neurotransmitters are chemicals secreted by each nerve cell to trigger receptors on the next nerve cell. Endorphins function something like oil in a machine. As with all hormones, they are released directly into the bloodstream and have rapid access to the brain. When endorphins come into contact with synapses, neurotransmitters transmit more effectively between cells. As a result, physical movement (especially exercise) makes our bodies feel refreshed and our brains more alert and in a better mood. This naturally improves our prayer.

Similar to walking, rocking the body stimulates it to a lesser degree. If you pray much with people who pray intensely, you will notice that they often rock their bodies without thinking about it. It is neither spiritual nor unspiritual to do this. It is a natural way that the brain is stimulated. God created us this way.

Brain and muscle stimulation is a good physiological reason to lift our hands and feet. Beyond that, lifting our limbs also brings the entire physical body into prayer. So let's get moving!

PRAYER
Starter

Lord, I lift my hands and eyes to you. I seek you with my whole heart, even my body. Fill me with your Spirit. . . .

— DAY 19 —

GUIDES OR NO GUIDES

I'm like most people—I forget things. When I pray a long
time, I usually think at some point, *Um, what should I pray
for next?* I need a list.

Kim does not use prayer lists. She flows with the Holy Spirit's
leading like a plane riding a jet stream. In extended times of
prayer with her, I wonder how she prays nonstop over more
things than a plane flies over in a coast-to-coast flight. I look
around for the list she must be hiding, but she has none. A list
would only get in her way.

It's up to you to determine what kind of person you are and
do what's appropriate. If your prayer flows like a river, or if you
pray in depth over one thing, stay away from guides. If not,
make one with me.

ONE WHO SYSTEMATICALLY PRAYED

Paul began letters to nearly every one of his churches and individuals with affirmations that he was praying for them. We see this in Romans 1:8–10; 1 Corinthians 1:4; Ephesians 1:16–23; Philippians 1:3–4; Colossians 1:3; 1 Thessalonians 1:2–3; 2 Timothy 1:3; and Philemon 4. A lot of references, I know, but they show how much he loved his people. Whether or not he used written lists, his letters reveal a leader who prayed systematically for his churches and church leaders.

The final greetings in most of Paul's letters mention individual workers. Those in Colossians and Romans give lots of attention to people Paul prayed for, and they read much like detailed prayer lists.

GUIDES AND LISTS THROUGH THE YEARS

As early as the fourth century, in the deserts of Egypt and the Holy Land, Evagrius Ponticus developed a prayer guide of pithy "sentences" (or "chapters") that followers read one at a time as subjects for prayer and meditation. For example, "The spirit that possesses health is the one which has no images of the things of this world at the time of prayer."[1] Or, "Reading, vigils and prayer—these are the things that lend stability to the wandering mind. Hunger, toil and solitude are the means of extinguishing the flames of desires."[2] He did well at integrating the mind and the spirit in a rigorous pattern of reflection. He showed us that sometimes reading and meditating on selections from Christian books benefits our time with God.

The early sixteenth-century founder of the Jesuits, Ignatius Loyola of Spain, compiled the *Spiritual Exercises*, which many still use today. It is a model of meditative prayer in which a person puts aside his or her own thoughts to focus on God. The disciplines guide people to read a scene from the Bible, usually one of the Gospels, and imagine themselves being there in that scene, aware of all their senses. What would they see? Hear? Smell? Feel? They imagine the scene as it was written—what was said and done—and contemplate what they themselves would say or do in that scene. Gospel stories come alive and impact readers when entered into this way. With any biblical story, you can stop and imagine yourself in the scene, the impact it would make on you, and how you would respond to God or to Jesus in the flesh. You may find it revitalizing.

Besides praying for the Holy Spirit's work in revival, Charles Finney's intercessor, Daniel Nash, made prayer lists of nonbelievers—you could call them spiritual hit lists. He often chose the most resistant, unlikely candidates for conversion, and many of them came to faith after his relentless intercession. Today many make lists as Nash did. And listing the hard-to-answer cases keeps us diligent to pray for people or things we might otherwise overlook.

PRAYER GUIDES

I recommend compiling a custom-made prayer guide. I've made a prayer notebook out of a three-ring binder, which enables me to add, remove, or rewrite notes, lists, or reminders. It's divided into several sections, and each is personalized as to what I'm committed to praying for—everything from my own character growth to world missions. I don't use it every day. But when I do, it gives structure and consistency to my prayer. I also have a highly abbreviated version in my wallet that I can pull out anytime. When I don't use it, I remember much of the content anyway, because I've used it so much.

Whatever size or shape your prayer guide takes, and whether it's paper or electronic, here are some suggestions for what you might include:

- *Written prayers or words of praise.* This will be helpful whenever you feel down or dull and need to crank your engine, as we saw in day 4.
- *Personal character growth.* Identify particular areas in which you need to grow. Character change and growth need constant reminding and affirming.
- *Personal commitments you've made.* This will help you be faithful to commitments you've made to yourself, to God, and to others.
- *Personal life vision and life goals.* This will keep you focused and on track with the big picture of what you see God doing in your life.
- *Needs of others.* This way when you say, "I'll pray for you," you can really mean it.
- *Your city, region, state, and nation.* Include governmental leaders, judges, current issues, or problems. Especially pray for the leaders you don't like.

- *Your local church.* Pray for your pastor, church leaders, members, children, ministries of the church, and unchurched people in your area.
- *World missions and missionaries, unreached peoples, and persecuted believers.* These are easy to forget, but in the big picture they're among the most important.
- *Answered prayer or things God has done.* Remembering God's answers will encourage you to be thankful and to keep praying.

You can use the Lord's Prayer as a guide by applying each phrase to your own life. Many people use the ACTS (or CATS) acronym: Adoration, Confession, Thanksgiving, and Supplication. If you're time oriented, you can do it by the clock: pray for something different every five minutes. Do whatever works for you.

Make use of different forms and patterns. Sometimes I open the contacts list in my cell phone and pray through the names.

SPONTANEITY

As great as prayer guides are, if you use them constantly they can become routine. If that happens, you may want to set your guide aside and pray spontaneously. I find that the more familiar I am with my lists, the more comprehensively I pray when I'm spontaneous. They seem to get engraved in my brain.

At times you will be pulled away from your guide for any number of good reasons. Some days you will have a pressing need to pray about. Other days God may inspire you to focus on one item out of your whole list.

If you are one who rarely or never uses guides, check yourself to see how comprehensive your prayer is and whether you should broaden it with a list. If you gravitate toward the same things all the time, you in fact have a built-in mental prayer list—it's just not on paper. And if you pray through all imaginable things, keep doing it. With or without guides, trust the Spirit to lead you.

PRAYER
~ *Starter* ~

Lord, lead me in what you would have me pray about. Help me to pray by the inspiration of your Spirit. . . .

— DAY 20 —

MINIMIZING DISTRACTIONS

Moses climbed Mount Sinai three times to fast and pray and talk to God (Exodus 19; 24; and 34). I can't help but think what a pain it must have been. Mount Sinai is a high, dry, forbidding rock pile. Climbing it is bad enough—why would anyone want to stay up there? The second and third times Moses hung out there for forty days. Why didn't he just stay in his tent of meeting where he normally talked with God (33:7)?

Jesus was no different. He wandered the Judean desert to fast for forty days. I've been to that desert. It's nothing but hills of dried-up rock and gravel—no wonder he met the devil there. No one else in their right mind would hang out in that place. Why didn't Jesus just go back to Capernaum, where his friends were? It was greener and prettier there. Or he could have fasted at the temple for forty days—at least it had shade.

When Moses received the Law and Jesus began his earthly ministry, they entered a period of total devotion to prayer. They each needed a place with no distractions. Every other place surrounded them with things to do, people's needs to meet, and decisions to make. When Moses and Jesus spent their forty days away from people, they banished distractions altogether.

DISTRACTIONS, DISTRACTIONS

"Every time I try to pray, my mind wanders." Have you ever said that? It happens to busy people. And multitaskers prize their ability to pretend they're two people at once. But in prayer that can be a problem. Serious connecting with God requires focus.

Distractions can surround us in the place we pray, and we'll catch ourselves saying, "This junk needs to be picked up," "I see another cobweb in the corner," or "What's that in the news?"

Distractions can come from thoughts floating, or taking up residence, in our minds. There's that call to make, that report to write, that gift to buy, that nagging question, that potential problem, and that project needing our attention. And they all have deadlines!

Distractions can come from the devil. Throughout the New Testament the devil continually sowed trouble in the minds of the disciples and church people.[1] Though he cannot know our thoughts as God does (he is a created being and not omniscient), he may throw thoughts into our minds disguised as our own thoughts. The devil often speaks in the first person singular: "I think . . ." "I want . . ." "I hate . . ." He will find a person's weak points and sow the temptation to indulge in lust, bitterness, deceit, backbiting, addictions, fears, or self-centeredness. He tailors temptations to maximize our likelihood of following the thoughts into sin and then feeling guilty for doing so. If you think you're a recipient of this, remember your identity as a child of God and command the thoughts to leave. Affirm that they have no part of your new nature.

DEAL WITH LOCATION

When the Roman emperor Constantine legalized Christianity in AD 313, the high cost of persecution for following Christ was slashed to the bargain of easy believing. Masses of people, often nominal in faith, came into the church, and leaders occasionally became self-indulgent. Monasticism, a movement of those who withdrew from society to devote themselves to prayer, simplicity, and solitude, arose as a reaction against the resulting worldliness of the church. Since serious believers no longer had persecution to purify them, many took to the rigors of austere self-denial in the desert. They feared becoming disconnected from God. So to keep their focus on God, they dealt with their prayer location in a big way—by moving to the middle of nowhere and living in caves to spare themselves the temptations of normal life.

You're probably not planning to become a desert hermit, and you're probably happy to pray at home. If you can practice intentional neglect, your home or workplace may be a good place to pray. But if you are tempted to clean every mess and attend to every task, another place might be better. As we saw in day 16, a location free of distractions can make a big difference in your prayer.

So if your location is prone to distractions, find a new one. At the very least, determine to neglect what would otherwise make you too busy to pray. Live with a little dirt or untidiness for a few minutes. Martha was a generous, responsible woman who opened her home to Jesus and the disciples. But she stressed out with things to do, while her sister Mary sat at Jesus' feet (Luke 10:38–42). Martha types are responsible and make things happen, but once in a while they need to join Mary.

DEAL WITH THE MIND

The desert hermits made an unfortunate discovery: though they avoided distractions of location, they couldn't escape distractions of the mind. Evagrius Ponticus, living in the deserts of Egypt and the Holy Land, wrote in the late fourth century: "Just as it is easier to sin by thought than by deed, so also is the war fought on the field of thought more severe than that which is conducted in the area of things and events. For the mind is easily moved indeed, and hard to control in the presence of sinful phantasies."[2] That's our consoling confirmation from an expert: the inside of our heads has more distractions than the outside.

Unlike changing our location, we can't pick a different brain. So what do we do when distracting thoughts invade our heads?

Yell, "God, help me focus!" That's a good start. Praying through a notebook or a prayer list also helps us to keep focused, because moving from one item to the next allows little room for our minds to wander, as we saw in day 19. It also helps to pray out loud, as we saw in day 12. Verbalizing our thoughts forces us to think coherently, which greatly reduces the mind's tendency to wander.

If you still catch your mind wandering, the following two sections may help you minimize distractions.

WRITE NOTES AND GO ON PRAYING

I keep notepaper and a pen handy during my prayer times. One reason is to write down impressions I receive from God (or at least think they're from him—a topic for day 28). Another reason is to write down thoughts that would otherwise nag me and hinder my focus.

If you suddenly remember that you need to buy something at the grocery store or make a phone call, you can distract yourself by trying not to forget it. Have you ever had your whole prayer time hindered by what you were trying not to forget? The solution is easy: jot a quick note to yourself, then forget about it as you go on praying.

Often in my prayer time, I think of all kinds of things to do on behalf of the people I pray for. (Most of my good ideas come either from my prayer time or from other people.) Many experience this quickening of the mind; it seems to be a benefit of uncluttered focus and of the Holy Spirit's presence. As ideas come, I jot them down. These notes often lead into action as a result of prayer. Since I first discovered this tendency, I've often planned my days or reviewed my plans during my God time. The thing to ask when doing this is, "Lord, what do you want me to do this day? This week? This month? This year?"

PRAY FOR THE THINGS THAT DISTRACT

What if God distracts you while you pray? That's called being led by the Holy Spirit. The Spirit may bring to your mind things or people to pray for. Or your mind may drift to concerns that need prayer. I've learned to accommodate the distraction into my flow of prayer. So instead of fighting myself over going on a tangent, I now pray about the tangential thought, then get back on track.

As you become more familiar with the Holy Spirit's leading, you will have times when the Holy Spirit impresses you to pray for something not on your list. Sometimes this can come with a sense of urgency. If you sense that, pray about it. The worst thing that could happen is that something will get extra prayer. The best thing is that you could unleash God's power through your prayer. You will also increase your sensitivity to the Spirit's leading and may begin to hear from God in ways you never expected.

If thoughts are lustful, selfish, or full of worry, don't quit praying! Confess them as part of your prayer. If you quit, you only give the devil a victory. And as we saw earlier, apart from your own sinful thoughts, he may try to toss his temptations into your mind. Then you may think how terrible you are to think those thoughts at all. Don't let the devil rob your intimacy with God and then make you feel guilty for it. Tell him to get lost.

Distractions or no distractions, may David's cry to God in Psalm 86:11 be ours as well: "Give me an undivided heart."

PRAYER
~ *Starter* ~

Lord, help me focus my thoughts on you. As I pray, my mind is open to receive anything you have to tell me. I give my attention to you alone. . . .

WINNING THE BATTLES

— *DAY 21* —

UNANSWERED PRAYER

Little Danny was two years old when he fell into the swimming pool. By the time his parents found him, he lay on the bottom. The EMTs resuscitated him, but the prolonged lack of oxygen left him in a coma, severely brain damaged. Danny was transferred to a developmental center, which is a nice term for a hospital where people stay until they die. He was on the second floor, which had a hall full of toddlers who had fallen into swimming pools. I've never seen more devoted mothers than I did there.

Every week or two Kim went there with Danny's mother and prayed for his healing. They cried. They claimed Scripture verses. They anointed with oil. But he wasn't healed. I went a few times and even celebrated his birthday. It's hard to have fun at a birthday party for a brain-damaged child who stares into space.

Danny grew more than a foot during the three years he lay in that bed. Kim prayed so hard.

Then Danny died.

Medically speaking, it was understandable, even expected.

Sometimes when people pour their guts out in faith, miracles trump science. But not always. Our church now has a ministry at that developmental center, but Kim says it's too painful for her to go back. It's been more than twenty years.

WHY DOESN'T GOD ANSWER?

We like to talk about how God answers prayer, but he has also *not* been answering—or answering no—for a long time. Psalms is full of bitter complaints to God for why he doesn't seem to answer prayer. King David writes: "How long, O LORD? Will you forget me forever? How long will you hide your face from me? How long must I wrestle with my thoughts and every day have sorrow in my heart? How long will my enemy triumph over me?" (Ps. 13:1–2).

Job, the Old Testament suffering guy, sat in misery and filed his objection to God's lack of response: "I will not keep silent; I will speak out in the anguish of my spirit, I will complain in the bitterness of my soul" (Job 7:11).

No praying person goes very far without wondering, sometimes screaming, "Why doesn't God answer me?" I think sometimes God decides to remind us he is God. Richard Foster says it well: "God, the great iconoclast, is constantly smashing our false images of who he is and what he is like. . . . In the very act of hiddenness God is slowly weaning us of fashioning him in our own image."[1] So by not answering our prayer, or by answering no, God may be graciously doing what we need. This may be why, amid the anguish he expresses above, David chooses faith and says in the same psalm, "But I trust in your unfailing love" (13:5).

Let me offer some possible reasons, in three categories, why we might not receive answer to prayer, or why the answer might be no.

HUMAN REASONS

Lack of faith. Lack of faith is a common reason for unanswered prayer. Though God responds to even a "mustard seed" of faith (Matt. 17:20), the Bible makes it clear that answers are according to our faith. Jesus lamented that his disciples did not have faith enough to cast out a demon (Mark 9:17–19). And before praying for Jairus's dead daughter, he sent the unbelieving people out of the room (Luke 8:49–56). They would apparently have hindered the reviving process. (But if taken superficially, this reason can also be abused and afflict people with undeserved guilt, especially those who are sick. Remember to have mercy!)

Sin. God will usually wait for us to confess sin before he answers prayer. James 5:16 says, "Confess your sins to each other and pray for each other so that you may be healed." When Jesus was confronted by the paralytic lowered through the roof, he did not say, "Be healed." He said, "Your sins are forgiven," and the man was healed (Mark 2:1–12). As if to nail us all, Psalm

66:18 states, "If I had cherished sin in my heart, the Lord would not have listened." Don't let sin take up residence!

Unforgiveness. Unforgiveness is one of countless sins, but it tends to stand out in unanswered prayer. Jesus makes it clear that if we do not forgive others who sin against us, the Father will likewise not forgive us (Matt. 6:14–15). And he instructed us that when we pray, if we have anything against anyone, we need to forgive that person so God will forgive our sins (Mark 11:25). Forgiving others goes a long way toward our prayers being answered.

Inner wounds. Inner wounds refer to afflictions on a person's emotions or psyche. Inner wounds most often occur in childhood and may result from parents' or other older people's indifference, overprotection, belittling, cursing, physical abuse, or sexual abuse. Inner wounds may also be inflicted throughout life. The death of a loved one or any great loss may cause inner wounds; rape is a terrible wound. Prayer for healing of inner wounds is often difficult and takes longer than that for physical wounds, because unlike the physical body, our psyche can talk back. People can be very resistant subconsciously to stepping out of entrenched coping mechanisms. Be aware of inner vows ("I will never . . ."); they have surprising power. Curses, addictions, and perversions may also pass down family lines and need to be revealed and broken before their effects can be overcome.[2]

Self-pity. I have never seen a person who consistently feels sorry for himself or herself receive much answer to prayer. An indulgent and twisted expression of compassion, self-pity is a form of sin. It can be subtle, seem justified, and feel good. But it denies the promises of God and short-circuits what he might otherwise do in us. Whether in ourselves or in others, self-pity must be dealt with sensitively but firmly. We cannot live in spiritual health with self-pity in our hearts.

Lifestyle. If we consistently eat unhealthy foods, smoke, drink, abuse drugs, never exercise, and are often stressed or angry, we will reap the results in a sick body. How can we expect the Lord to heal us if our habits make us sick again? If our values and habits are not in line with Scripture, how can we ask the Lord to bless us? For him to do so would be contrary to his Word.[3] We need our whole lifestyle to be in agreement with our prayers.

The pray-er. Sometimes one person prays and nothing happens, then someone else prays and God answers. While all are called to pray, some have spiritual gifts of faith, healing, or miraculous powers (1 Cor. 12:9–10). If the Holy Spirit is particularly active someplace, we may want to check it out. But that does not necessarily mean chasing after big-name people or events. And as we pray, we also need to check our intentions. James 4:3 says, "You do not receive, because you ask with wrong motives." Those who ask God's blessings in order to share them receive more than those who ask blessings in order to hoard them.

DEMONIC REASONS

Demonization. "Demonization" is a transliteration of the Greek word *daimonzai* used throughout the New Testament. Neither "possession" nor "obsession" is true to the actual biblical usage. Demonic influence comes in degrees, not in simple black and white. I probably don't need to explain that demons can hinder prayer, whether with the one praying or with the one receiving prayer. And as frightening as demons may be, fear is a waste of energy. Believers have authority over demons, and amazing things happen when we exercise it. (See day 25 for more on this.)

Affliction. Demons can in no way possess someone who is reborn by the Spirit of God. But our bodies are not reborn like our spirits; that will happen at the final resurrection (1 Cor. 15:42–44). Demons can physically afflict believers. For eighteen years Satan physically afflicted a daughter of Abraham (one who has received salvation; see Luke 19:9) until Jesus delivered her (Luke 13:10–16).

On the nonphysical side, the battle is in the soul—a person's mind, will, and emotions. In the three-part understanding of body, soul, and spirit (1 Thess. 5:23; Heb. 4:12), our souls are not instantly reborn as a new creation the way our spirits are (2 Cor. 5:17). Our souls mature and become Christlike (v. 16). That is also where our struggles are. Satan asked to sift Peter as wheat, and apparently Jesus allowed him to (Luke 22:31–32). Jesus rebuked Satan as he spoke through Peter (Matt. 16:22–23). Ananias and Sapphira were believers, but Satan had filled their hearts (Acts 5:1–11). Recognizing and resisting Satan's infiltration can be a big step toward answered prayer.

Strongholds. A stronghold is "an entrenched pattern of thought, an ideology, value or behavior that is contrary to the word and will of God."[4] Second Corinthians 10:5 describes strongholds as "arguments and every pretense that sets itself up against the knowledge of God." Non-Christians usually have strongholds; otherwise they would turn to Christ. But Christians can also hold unbiblical or ungodly thoughts, ideologies, values, or behaviors. Paul adds in the above passage that "we take captive every thought to make it obedient to Christ." The most common spiritual battle is for the mind.

GODLY REASONS

Working behind the scenes. Have you ever questioned whether God was even listening—then discovered that the entire time he was arranging the preliminaries to answer your prayer? God often works incognito. Recalling the parting of the Red Sea for Moses and the Israelites, Asaph expresses how God acts without us being aware: "Your path led through the sea, your way through the mighty waters, though your footprints were not seen" (Ps. 77:19). God may be protecting us, and we don't realize it—I sometimes imagine the terrible things that could happen to me but don't. God may be going ahead of our prayer, attending to the details necessary for the life change we seek. God may be waiting for the right time to answer. Sometimes the best thing we can do is patiently trust God, even though we might not have a clue what he's doing.

Chastisement. I'd be careful before telling someone that God punishes people and doesn't answer their prayer, but it happens. When Saul grew angry and jealous toward David, "an evil spirit from God came forcefully upon Saul" (1 Sam. 18:10). Gehazi, assistant to the prophet Elisha, was afflicted with leprosy as punishment for his greed (2 Kings 5:20–27). In 1 Corinthians 11:29–30 Paul says that anyone who takes communion without recognizing the body of the Lord "eats and drinks judgment on himself. That is why many among you are weak and sick, and a number of you have fallen asleep [died]." It's harsh, but we need to remember that God is, well, God.

God's classroom. To keep him humble after his rapture to heaven, Paul says, "There was given me a thorn in my flesh, a messenger of Satan, to torment me" (2 Cor. 12:7). Paul pleaded with God to take it away, but he did not. Instead he taught Paul humility and that his power operates in human weakness. In the end Paul was glad (vv. 7–10). God readily teaches us when we are ready to learn—and sometimes when we're not.

Testing and faith building. Job's afflictions were one big test. God sometimes tests us to see what we're made of. Because it's easy to live on blessings, God may use unanswered prayer to build our faith, as in, "Will you trust me even if you don't get what you want?" These are times when God allows us to become desperate in order to draw us closer to him and grow in faith. It's similar to growth rings on a cross section of a tree. The thin, dark parts of each ring form when the tree endures a dry season or a cold winter. That part of the ring is hard and is what makes the tree, and the lumber it yields, strong. The same is true in our own lives.

Old age and death. Some ailments are a fact of old age. Our bodies are designed to wear out—which guarantees that we exit this place called earth. Whenever I enter a hospital's intensive care unit or pray for someone gravely ill, I ask God outright, "Is this sickness (or injury) unto death?" I want to receive God's leading on how to pray. As much as I've seen miraculous healings, every person still has a time to die, and I don't want to fight God.

A GOD VIEW

If God always answered our prayers right away, most of us would treat him like a cosmic ATM machine—put prayer in, get answer out. We'd be brats. If unanswered prayer doesn't drive us away from God, it will draw us nearer to him—perhaps God's greatest desire. The vision of Revelation 5:8 depicts prayer as incense in bowls held before God. The vision is revisited in 8:3–5, where incense (prayer) has long accumulated and is offered on the altar before God's throne, followed by a dramatic heaven's-eye view of answered prayer. It's in the extended longing, the pleading of his promises, that we draw near to God—and ultimately receive the answer he knows is best.

When all else fails, and still nothing makes sense, four words remain: "I do not know." Romans 8:28 can help here: "In all things God works for the good of those who love him, who have been called according to his purpose." When we don't know, at least we can trust.

PRAYER
~ *Starter* ~

Lord, you're not answering my prayer, and I'm struggling. Help me to know why so I can deal with it. And even if I don't know why, I commit myself into your hands and trust your faithfulness for the ultimate good. . . .

— *DAY 22* —

THE WRESTLING RING

I wanted my church to grow. A big congregation would glorify God and make me feel fulfilled. So I went to seminars and read books on how to increase my numbers. And I did what they told me.

I paced circles around the sanctuary and prayed. I quietly listened; I cried out. Then the Lord seemed to say, *Do you want a big church, or do you want me?*

I knew the correct answer.

He went on: *What if no one else showed up for worship on Sunday morning and you were the only one here? If only I were here, would that be okay with you?*

Why did God pick *me* for this question? Grudgingly I said, "Yes, Lord. Even if you were the only one here on Sunday morning, that would be okay with me." I hoped he wouldn't take me up on that.

I had to lose the battle. I had to let go of my will and subordinate my desires to God's. Only then could I receive his will as being my own. He must have been pleased, because the following Sunday was one of the most Spirit-filled, prayer-answered Sundays I could remember.

Weeks later I experienced one of those flashing God moments. While waiting for a meeting to start at another church facility, I wandered around and poked my head into the sanctuary just to check it out. An immaculate seven-hundred-seat suburban pastor's dreamland spread before me. I thought, *Do I envy this? Do I want this kind of sanctuary and the ministry that goes with it?* For most of my pastoral life and for most pastors, it's a no-brainer: of course! But in an instant, from the depth of my gut, I said, "No. I do not need this. I no longer crave it. If I get it, fine. But what I want is God's presence—even if our church doesn't grow, even if we meet in a warehouse." At that instant I knew I had lost the struggle and was on my way to something good. I had a deep peace after that—and our church even grew.

LINING UP WILLS

The Bible makes a mind-blowing promise in 1 John 5:14–15, and most of us never take it seriously: "If we ask anything according to his will, he hears us. And if we know that he hears us—whatever we ask—we know that we have what we asked of him." Which basically means that God will listen if we pray in line with what he wants, and then he will give us what we ask. This also implies that when we pray contrary to God's will, he won't hear us, and we won't get what we ask. He's God, so I suppose he can do that. And the most important thing we can do when we pray is find out what his will is, then pray according to it—which should be okay for us, because he has our best interests in mind. So I have a question: why do most of us just dive into prayer and say what *we* want without seriously considering what God might want?

Sometimes it's hard to get in line with what God wants. He might want us to wait, sacrifice, or do something that seems crazy. But we want to close the business deal now, get every option we can, and make the safe decision that experts advise. That's when we wrestle in prayer. We wrestle when our human desires clash with God's desires. Here's the unavoidable point: we cannot get what we want until we let go and align ourselves with him. When his will becomes ours, we get answers to prayer.

My seminary's housing department offered me a full-time, full-benefits job, and I was ready to take it. Then I prayed about it. God seemed to blast me with anxiety and the inescapable notion that I should instead take a position as a youth pastor for two-thirds the salary and no benefits. I did *not* like the idea. I wrestled in prayer for a week. God wouldn't let up, so I gave in and did the youth pastor stint. Fast forward a year. I tallied all the personal checks that parents had given me out of thanks for what I did with their kids, the fact that I never needed the medical benefits, and the results of lives changed in that youth group. I found that I was ahead in every way for having taken the youth pastor job.

This same pattern can work with anything. It's like a dad tussling with his little kid. To get ourselves in tune with God, we often wrestle. Like the dad, God could crush us (the kid). But he goes along with our wrestling until—if we're willing—we submit and lose. After that he takes what we're grappling with and turns it into our benefit.

WRESTLING WITH GOD

In the years before tacking up his 95 Theses, Martin Luther wrestled with God all the time. Chafing under church traditions and theology, he often anguished over his own salvation and how to relate to an almighty God. He underwent long fasts, confessions, and prayer vigils. He often grew distressed over the corrupt state of the church and the condition of his own soul. This very process of wrestling with God (and with false concepts of God) led to his breakthrough and to the Protestant Reformation.

Wrestling with God is not something most of us need to do all the time. But once in a while we need to. Wrestling with God happens when, at the deepest level, we bring ourselves and our desires into full, tumultuous interaction with God. It happens when we sense his leading but we're not sure we want to follow. Or maybe the Bible seems impossible to obey. So we struggle.

The Bible is full of people who struggled: Moses with the unruly Israelites, Job with his afflictions, David with Saul, Joseph with his role as the Savior's dad, Paul with his thorn in the flesh. If you wrestle with God, you're in good company.

I eventually made a discovery about this wrestling: it is actually with ourselves as much as with God. It is grappling with the pride of our own wills, with the weakness of our human nature, and with the ingrained ways life has programmed in us. In that way of seeing it, God is just playing along, patiently dealing with us until we pray and act the way he knows is best.

THE PENIEL WRESTLING RING

At a place he named Peniel (meaning "face of God"), Jacob wrestled with an angel, a mysterious "man" who identified himself as representing God (Gen. 32:22–32). The angel condescended to wrestle with Jacob but "saw that he could not overpower him" (v. 25). Jacob was so tenacious that the angel had to wrench Jacob's hip from its socket to make him let go. This supernatural display of power, the mere touch upon Jacob's hip that wrenched it and made him limp, tells us that the angel could have easily overpowered Jacob. So how could the angel not subdue him, yet overcome him with a mere touch?

The physical struggle (which the angel easily won) was not the core of the conflict. The main issue was the psychological battle—the struggle of will and faith. The test was how much tenacity Jacob had. This encounter lasted all night until the angel finally had enough and told Jacob, "You have struggled with God and with men and have overcome" (v. 28). The angel won the physical match, but Jacob "overcame" him in the sense that he refused to give up. He said, "I will not let you go unless you bless me" (v. 26). He passed the test and received his blessing.

This question comes to us: do we have the will, the faith, and the tenacity to overcome unanswered prayer and difficult situations? From our guts, will we say to God, "I will not let you go unless you bless me"?

THE GETHSEMANE WRESTLING RING

In the Garden of Gethsemane, Jesus' humanity came through so much it frightens me. Believers in Jesus know him as the risen Lord and Lord of the universe, before whom every knee will bow. But in the garden he struggled. He wrestled as a man wrestles with God. Three times he prayed intensely over whether or not he would really go through with the tortured-to-death-on-the-cross scenario (Matt. 26:36–44). Here Jesus was as human as we ever see him. Did he actually say he did not want to die on the cross? Yes, he did.

During this encounter an angel came from heaven to strengthen him—and he wrestled even harder (Luke 22:43–44). This amazes me: God the Father *helped* Jesus to wrestle with him. If the same is true for us, in the very struggles we have with God, he actually helps us to grapple with him until it's over. God knows the value of wrestling in prayer. He must see it more clearly from the other side.

Jesus' manhood and godhood wrestled so intensely that, as physicians describe it, the capillaries in his skin ruptured. When that happens, blood leaks like sweat from the pores. Normally that happens only with head injuries, strangulations, or when people hang upside down for a long time. Luke 22:44 says that

Jesus' "sweat was like drops of blood falling to the ground." Here's a thought: no one ever wrestled with God in prayer as intensely as Jesus himself did. From that point of view, wrestling in prayer is not disobeying God—it's a way to be like Jesus.

Look at what happened to Jesus after this wrestling. He totally subordinated himself to the Father's will and took the "not my will but yours be done" position. From then on he was unflinching when arrested, he was in control before Pilate, and he was unflagging all the way to his cruel death. How do we know? While being arrested, he healed a man's ear. When he stood before Pilate, Pilate was the nervous one. And throughout the entire time on the cross, Jesus could have called a platoon of angels to blast away all the bad guys. But he chose not to.

EARLY CHURCH WRESTLING RINGS

Paul wrestled with God. In his letter to the Philippians, he says, "I desire to depart [die] and be with Christ . . . but it is more necessary for you that I remain" (1:23–24). Paul didn't mind getting life over with and going to heaven, but he knew that God, or at least the people, needed him on earth a while longer. So he grappled over his desire versus God's will and ultimately submitted to God's will—which then became his own.

In his letter to the Colossians, Paul relays greetings from Epaphras, who "is always wrestling in prayer for you" (4:12). The Greek word used here for "wrestle" is *agonizomai*, which is the origin of our word "agonize." It can also be translated "struggle" or "fight" and is used in athletic contests to mean "compete" or "do one's best." That is how Epaphras prayed—with an all-out effort, a physical workout complete with conflict and agony. Don't ever let anyone tell you that prayer is for wimps.

LOSE TO WIN

I hope you will wrestle with God. And I hope that you will lose and surrender your own will to your heavenly Father. By losing to him, you will win.

PRAYER
~ *Starter* ~

> Lord, I'm struggling with [name the issue]. As
> I wrestle, lead me into conformity with you,
> and make your will my own. . . .

— *DAY 23* —

SPRINTS AND MARATHONS

A three-year-old girl, whom I'll call Brittany, loved to play, but her knees would ache. She continually cried out, "My knees hurt!" She often collapsed from the pain and couldn't even walk. Doctors could not diagnose her illness.

One year her homeschooling group put on a Christmas play, and she played an angel. But during a practice she collapsed again. At the end of the rehearsal, the director called out, "Kids, let's pray for Brittany." The children gathered around her and laid hands on her knees. Each one prayed simple, one- or two-sentence prayers.

When all had prayed, Brittany jumped up and said, "Let's go play on the slide!" The illness never returned.

Prayer can be like a sprint and receive an answer when some-one seizes an opportunity.

Brittany's parents, whom I'll call Bill and Molly, had been married for fifteen and a half years, and most of that time they fought. Their two older daughters told Molly, "Get a divorce." But four-year-old Brittany remained quiet. She began to pray silently every night at bedtime. For three full years she wouldn't tell what she prayed, and she wouldn't stop praying.

After eighteen and a half years of marital turmoil, Bill and Molly finally agreed to divorce. On Christmas Eve they went to bed, bitter as always. On Christmas morning, Molly awoke and looked at Bill. Her bitterness was gone. She felt only love, and she didn't know why. Bill's bitterness had also vanished. And he didn't know why, but he felt he was in love with Molly again. They had no explanation—until Brittany, now seven, saw them and thanked God for answering her silent prayer of three years and doing a miracle in her mommy's and daddy's hearts by making them love each other again.

Prayer can be like a marathon, demanding patient endurance.

Sprints

The most edgy people I've ever known were some of my high school track teammates: the sprinters. Nerves on edge, their whole bodies twitched every day we had a meet. From morn-ing until afternoon they keyed up for the starting gun. The race could be won or lost by their reflexes off the blocks. Then they had to run like the wind toward the finish line, only seconds away. If they lost any opportunity, they lost the race.

I sometimes think of the opportunities I have seized to pray. Then I think of opportunities I've lost. Lost opportunities are harder to pinpoint—after all, I missed them. It seems that capturing or missing prayer opportunities largely depends on two things: alertness and boldness. When I was alert and bold, I prayed a lot more than when I wasn't.

Alertness means I'm aware of what's going on around me and I have an attitude prepared to pray—the way a sprinter is attentive to the starting gun. When I face a problem at work, I'm quick to talk to God about it. When I see a hurting or troubled person, I offer to help and pray. But when I'm not alert, it means I *don't* see. I don't help and I don't pray. Lack of alertness may cause a lack of concern for others, but I think it's usually the other way around. If my thoughts center on myself and my agenda, as they easily can on busy days, I don't have room to put others' needs first, which means I'm also unlikely to pray for them. I find that more than training or skill, my *attitude* is important whether I serve or pray for others.

Boldness means I don't fear what others think, because I'm more interested in meeting a need, whether my own or someone else's. The bolder I am, the more opportunities I will seize. When I miss opportunities to pray, I often find in me a lack of boldness. I can feign anything from humility to sophistication. But deep down it's more likely a lack of confidence, fear of what others think, or not caring much about other people. Boldness, motivated by love, seizes chances when they arise.

Every day offers countless opportunities to pray for those who don't even know we're praying: a missionary in central Asia, victims in today's headline, or the wounded in ambulances screaming by. Plenty of times when I was young and ready for trouble, it seemed that trouble went the other way. Years later I found that my mother habitually prayed for me when I went out. Her talking to God worked a lot better than nagging me ever could have. Like a sprinter, she was quick to pray when needs arose. And when I care for others as she has for me, I'll be alert enough to seize chances as they come.

MARATHONS

I was a long-distance runner. Skinny guys like me had little other racing opportunities. If we were slow at the starting gun, no problem; the race was long enough to catch up—if we didn't twist an ankle, cringe with blisters, or keel over from cramps. One year I ran a marathon—26 miles, 385 yards (42.2 kilometers)—the distance a Greek messenger in 490 BC ran to Athens with a victory report from a battle site at Marathon. (I wonder what kind of shoes he had.) A marathoner must endure not only physically but also mentally. I was ready to drop out halfway through the race. But my brain yelled threats and kept my legs moving until the finish line.

Similarly, when we pray, our endurance is largely mental. A long-distance pray-er has the tenacity not to give up in the face of seemingly unanswered prayer. I say "seemingly" because God may be working behind the scenes in a way we don't expect.

Through all the ups and downs of my childhood, teen, and college years, my mother did her best to put up with me and never stopped praying that I would get right with God. Neither she nor I knew it, but God worked in my life throughout those twenty-one years, until one night, halfway around the world when I was an exchange student in Japan, I opened up and received Jesus as Lord of my life.

God gives us a privilege reserved for royalty when he tells us we can boldly approach him at his throne of grace (Heb. 4:16). He also declares that we have authority over demonic powers and sickness (Matt. 10:1). But God has never given us license over other people's hearts and minds. So we will always deal with challenges of ungodly thoughts and behaviors, what the Bible calls "the flesh" or "sinful nature." Sometimes we find it in others, sometimes in us.

Here I return to Epaphras, the guy who was "always wrestling in prayer" for the Colossians (Col. 4:12). He contended for the Colossian believers' faith and maturity, and as a marathoner, he wouldn't give up on them. When we pray for people, sometimes we need to be ready for marathons.

Prayer requests can stretch into weeks, months, or years because of sin, spiritual warfare, or being out of line with God's will. So I've wondered, if all these factors determine the outcome, and if our sovereign God has his will made up, why pray at all? I concluded that it's because he chooses to work through us. He's a dad. So he insists that we participate in what he's doing. I'm a dad too, and I won't do everything for my kid; that's the worst thing I could do. I want her to participate, because that's how she grows up.

Sometimes it seems that God will not do anything unless we participate. So I keep praying.

HEROINES OF PRAYER

The lady with the twelve-year hemorrhage in Mark 5:25–34 is a heroine of sprinting prayer. She saw a chance to touch Jesus as he passed by. Jewish law considered her "unclean" because of her bleeding, so she risked punishment by sneaking up in the crowd to touch Jesus' robe. She seized the chance anyway. And at that instant her faith healed her. Jesus is looking for sprinters—those who are quick to pray when needs or opportunities arise.

The widow of Jesus' parable in Luke 18:1–8 is a heroine of marathon prayer. She relentlessly bothered the judge—drove him nuts—until she got justice. Jesus literally invites us to "cry out to him day and night" (v. 7). He's looking for marathon-ers—not those who are able but those who are willing.

PRAYER
~ *Starter* ~

Lord, move me to be caring and alert enough to seize opportunities to pray. And keep me faithful—tenacious—in praying for things that take a long time to be answered. . . .

— DAY *24* —

PERSISTENT BOLDNESS

Ronnie was a defensive tackle for his high school football team. In the state playoffs, a 325-pound lineman smashed into Ronnie's knee and did some terrible damage to the joint. From November through May, he limped in pain. Every day he iced his knee and wrapped it in elastic bandages. And he kept limping. Ronnie also prayed every day but saw no healing. He was discouraged. He doubted whether God would ever heal him or whether God even heard him.

I went with Ronnie to the best orthopedic surgeon in Los Angeles and saw the X-ray of his knee. It clearly showed the torn cartilage sticking out of the knee joint. Surgery was too expensive for the family, and I encouraged him to pray hard—the way he played football. We read Philippians 4:6–7, which says not to worry about anything but to bring our requests to God, whose peace would guard our hearts and minds. With preseason training only two months away, we asked God to give Ronnie peace about whether he would play or not play. Ronnie clearly sensed God telling him he would play that fall. We boldly prayed and expected his healing. But the pain still racked his knee. He grew confused and sometimes discouraged. We kept praying and trusting anyway. Then one morning in June, he awoke to find his knee completely healed.

He played football that fall and made it through the entire season with no problems in his healed knee. We were thankful for an answer to prayer yet unprepared for how far it would go: in the defensive tackle position, Ronnie was voted player of the year for the entire Southern California league.

NOT TOO POLITE, PLEASE

We naturally want God to be happy when we pray, and many of us figure we'd better be polite. Of course we should be respectful when we pray; this is the master of the universe we're talking to. But I wonder if God sometimes gets bored with us. Does our civility become diplomatic, ceremonial, even wimpy? It may seem impolite to demand or cry out. Yet the Bible never teaches us to pray politely.

Most prayers in the Bible, especially the New Testament, are straight to the point. The Psalms are home to moaning prayers that can get downright nasty. R. A. Torrey says, "God delights in the holy boldness that will not take no for an answer. It is an expression of great faith, and nothing pleases God more than faith."[1] That's it. Boldness that doesn't give up is evidence of faith. Jesus shows little interest in what we sound like. He tries to get our attention with strong examples in which he goes all the way and tells us to be obnoxious. We may offend him with our sin, but never with our boldness.

Jesus makes his point in Luke 11:5–8 with the parable of the friend at midnight. (At least that's what preachers and Bible editors call it. I call it the parable of the obnoxious dude at midnight.) Jesus says what if a guy goes to his friend's house at *midnight*, bangs on the door, and asks for not one but three—*three*—loaves of bread to give to his out-of-town guest? What is wrong with this guy? Of course the one inside shouts back that the door is locked and he's in bed trying to sleep, so go away. Their friendship (probably strained at this point) is not enough to drag him out of bed. But the bold audacity of the door-banger dude finally rouses this poor guy out of bed to "give him [the friend] as much as he needs" (v. 8). And we're supposed to take that as an example of how to pray.

Jesus immediately follows the story of the obnoxious friend with a statement that most Bible translations miss—the ask, seek, and knock thing (Luke 11:9–10). The verb tense of the original Greek is more like, "*Continually* ask and it will be given to you; *continually* seek and you will find; *continually* knock and the door will be opened to you." Repetition is part of being obnoxious, and Jesus asks for it. I struggle to imagine why he likes to hear us bug him. But as with every other way God is involved in our lives, this is for our own good.

Look again at the parable of the persistent widow in Luke 18:1–5. (I'd rather call it the parable of the lady who wouldn't give up or shut up or take no for an answer.) She who was socially destitute took on a powerful, amoral judge who couldn't have cared less about her, anyone else, or even God. He refused to help her and brought no justice against her adversary. She had absolutely nothing going for her except her bold audacity to approach him and her obnoxious persistence to do it every single day. The judge finally decided to bring justice only because she bothered him ceaselessly: "Grant me justice. Grant me justice. Grant me justice. Grant me justice. Grant me justice."

Jesus then says, "Will not God bring about justice for his chosen ones, who cry out to him day and night? . . . He will see that they get justice" (Luke 18:7–8). But here's the rub: Jesus finishes by saying, "However, when the Son of Man comes, will he find faith on the earth?" (v. 8). He is essentially asking, "Does anyone around here have faith to pray like that?"

When you have a legitimate need, Jesus literally invites you, urges you, to pray with persistent boldness. Bang on heaven's door, even if it seems obnoxious, and with bold faith make your request. Pray God's ear off like the persistent widow. I wonder if God is weary and bored with centuries of polite, religious prayers. I think all of us can find room to be more bold and persistent.

Parents can understand this. Small children aren't the least bit concerned how respectable their requests sound to their parents. When they decide what they want, they let Mom or Dad know—over and over and over and over. When my daughter was six, she wanted to go to the park almost every day. She would bug me and bug me and bug me and bug me. I didn't always go with her just because she was my beloved daughter; I had work to do. Sometimes I went with her because I was miserable if I didn't. So I brought my office work and cell phone with me to the park bench. God actually *wants* us to pray like a kid who pesters Mom and Dad. If the cross is not proof enough of God's love for us, then surely this invitation to pester him is!

BOLDLY BUG GOD

In 1892 John Hyde, a Presbyterian missionary, sailed to India, a rock-hard mission field with few converts. Like other missionaries, Hyde struggled with the language and with telling uninterested people about Jesus. Discouragement drove him to pray hard. By 1899 he was spending entire nights in prayer. Starting in 1904 his zeal for God and prayer spread to his missionary colleagues. Then in 1908 he dared to pray for what seemed inconceivable: one person somewhere within the mission work to come to faith every day. *Impossible*, most thought. But in one year four hundred people came to Christ. A year later Hyde felt led by God to double his request: two conversions a day. That year saw eight hundred conversions. By 1910 he felt God leading him to pray for four conversions a day, and the growth continued.

John Hyde prayed day and night, often going without food or sleep. He shouted and wept and often said, "Give me souls, O God, or I die!" Sometimes Hyde prayed "for thirty days and nights, or ten days on end, or remain[ed] on his knees for thirty-six hours without moving."[2] God not only brought hundreds to salvation but also sent revival to the mission churches. Hyde prayed so intensely for so long that in the end his body gave out from exhaustion—he virtually prayed himself to death.

If you're thinking, *No way*, so am I. But this guy was for real. People like him may come along once every one hundred years, but rather than feeling that I stink by comparison, I've decided to let Hyde be one of my heroes of persistent boldness. Even if I manage 10 percent of what he did, his crazy-man example encourages me.

I think we all need that encouragement, because sometimes it seems as if God's not listening. That's when we need persistence. I've noticed that God has a tendency to test what our faith and hearts are made of. Besides that, when he seems not to listen, we often pray more, and that brings us closer to him—his ultimate aim. In time the answers will come.

The Lord says to the Israelites through the prophet Isaiah that they haven't yet worn themselves out bugging him: "You have not called upon me, O Jacob, you have not wearied yourselves for me, O Israel" (Isa. 43:22). Even more pointedly, he commands pray-ers to pester him: "You who call on the LORD, give yourselves no rest, and give him no rest till he establishes Jerusalem and makes her the praise of the earth" (62:6–7). Almost like a coach, God looks for players who give everything they've got when they pray.

After praying with countless people, I have come to believe that many of us use the sovereignty of God as an excuse. (Don't get me wrong; I believe in the sovereignty of God. And let's remember that John Hyde was a sovereignty-of-God-believing Presbyterian.) As spiritual as it may appear, some may consign everything to the sovereignty of God as an easy out to cover laziness, complacency, and lack of passion. Can we really speak of the sovereignty of God without the involvement of humankind? God has sovereignly chosen to work through us. If we do not give ourselves fully, how much can we expect from God?

Too often we pray, assume God got it, quit praying, and go on with our busy day. If we get no answer, we might assume that something must not be God's will, when in reality we didn't boldly persist. The people I see who consistently yield great fruit through their prayers are people who battle in prayer not for a few moments but for days. This is the continual seeking, continual asking, and continual knocking Jesus speaks of in Matthew 7:7 and Luke 11:9–10. And our God-coach is ready to help us pray that way.

PRAYER
~ Starter ~

Lord, too often I've slacked off in my prayer. I commit this time to praying the way you desire. Motivate me to be bold and persistent as I pray. . . .

— DAY 25 —

THE GREAT WAR

I encountered an uninvited demon while I was in seminary and leading a Bible study in Los Angeles. A twentysomething woman was fidgeting and grimacing. When I talked to her, she glared at me, wrinkled her nose, and sneered. Then others in the Bible study tried to talk to her, and she growled at them in a low, gravelly voice. We started praying for her, but she pushed us aside and crouched on all fours underneath a table. The other folks looked at me—the seminary student who was supposed to be able to do something. But I'd only read about this stuff.

I figured we should start by pulling her out from under the table. I picked the three biggest people there—big guys, mind you—and we each took an arm or a leg. This should not have been a problem, because the woman was one of the skinniest people I'd ever seen. When I grabbed her upper arm, my thumb and index finger could touch. We pulled her out without any problems. Then with superhuman strength she threw off all four of us at once. We tumbled back, and she crawled back under the table, leered at us, and growled in that low, gravelly voice.

It took two days to set her free from the demon. We learned a lot.

SPIRITUAL WARFARE

Welcome to the war. Some of us have less dramatic encounters, but no one goes untouched. We humans are capable of causing most of the problems in the world. But throughout Scripture we also see descriptions of spiritual powers of evil influencing people's minds and behaviors. We see the war throughout the church's history too: controversies over heresy, struggles in missionary advances, and persecution by totalitarian governments. In our own culture we see kids (or parents) gone astray, immorality, paganism, corruption, crime, broken families, and splintered churches. Behind much of this, some kind of spiritual influence usually lurks—"the spirit who is now at work in those who are disobedient," as Ephesians 2:2 says of Satan.

Spiritual warfare can be defined as any confrontation with spiritual powers of evil. Or we can look at 1 Peter 5:8–9: "Be self-controlled and alert. Your enemy the devil prowls around like a roaring lion looking for someone to devour. Resist him, standing firm in the faith." From these verses we could define spiritual warfare as recognizing and resisting the devil's schemes.

Colossians 2:15 says, "Having disarmed the powers and authorities, he [Jesus] made a public spectacle of them, triumphing over them by the cross." Some people will cite this verse and say that Jesus already defeated the powers of evil on the cross, so we don't have to do spiritual warfare. How I wish that were true. But that is like saying since Jesus sacrificed his life for us on the cross to give us salvation, we don't have to repent or receive Christ. Any true follower of Jesus would say, "That's ridiculous!" Spiritual warfare is the same. In order to benefit a person, Jesus' finished work on the cross—whether salvation or spiritual warfare—must be received and lived out in that person's life.

THE CONFLICT

I asked myself why the Bible says, "We know that we are children of God, and that the whole world is under the control of the evil one" (1 John 5:19). I started to see that if we as believers want to avoid defeat in our struggles, it helps to know two things: our identity and the world's identity. Evil gains influence through spirits deceiving people and through habits of sin (lust, greed, pride, laziness, anger, selfishness, violence, power-mongering, thievery), but it also makes inroads through worldly systems (religious, social, political, economic). People, on the other hand, gain a new identity by connecting with Jesus. John 1:12 says, "To all who received him, to those who believed in his name, he gave the right to become children of God." The word for "right" can also be translated "power" or "authority." That's good news when we consider the evil we're up against across the planet.

Spiritual conflict in the lives of believers is not between our new spiritual identity and our old spiritual identity. The battle is between our new self and the sinful nature (the ingrained patterns of ungodly thinking and behaving). Demonic temptations come on top of this. The Holy Spirit inhabits believers, which means that believers can never be "possessed" by a demon. But believers can still be deceived or afflicted by evil spirits. I know many Christians don't like to believe that, but see Matthew 16:23; Luke 13:16; 22:31; John 13:27; Acts 5:3; and 2 Corinthians 11:3. Those passages make it clear that believers can be influenced or oppressed. Yet plenty of other verses show us that we don't have to be, such as Romans 8:5, 13; 1 Corinthians 10:13; Titus 2:12; and 1 John 4:1.

Here's the hard news: since the whole world lies under the control of the evil one, spiritual warfare involves everyone alive. We don't have a choice about whether a war goes on around us. Our choice is whether to engage in it and win.

Two cautions: First, please do not make a habit of doing spiritual warfare carelessly. The devil lashes back in all sorts of ways. Be right with God. Have others pray for you. Pray for God's protection. We have no need to fear, but we're smart to take the conflict seriously. Second, I don't recommend engaging in spiritual warfare if you have deep emotional wounds. The devil tends to afflict emotionally damaged people as it is; going into battle would only make it worse. You need healing and deliverance first.

For a head-on statement about spiritual warfare, see Ephesians 6:10–18. It's a bit long to quote here, but it majors on taking our stand against the devil's schemes, recognizing that the battle is spiritual not physical, maintaining the right spiritual disposition (the "armor of God"), and praying at all times. It's written to believers in the church—people like us. Our struggles are ultimately not against "flesh and blood," as in the government, a spouse, or the people at work. And our conflict—hear this—is not with non-Christians. It's with a vast array of evil spirits. Thankfully, the Bible does not tell us to study about demons or chase them. But it doesn't tell us to ignore them either. And, contrary to Hollywood movies, it does *not* tell us to fear them. The Bible says, "Put on the full armor of God" and "take your stand" (v. 11). Them's fightin' words.

Remember to recognize and resist (1 Peter 5:8–9). We recognize by discerning where spiritual powers might have influence. We resist by taking a stand, as Ephesians 6:11–14 says four times. We can take a stand against any evil power behind afflictions on ourselves, our family, our loved ones, our church, our city, our nation, or other parts of the world. We can say no to the devil and yes to God. Sometimes it's a long fight, but we can expect to win. We win when we pray and obey.

TWO LEVELS

Spiritual warfare can take place at what we might call "ground level," when we confront powers of evil that influence, oppress, or afflict individual people. The demonized people whom Jesus freed and healed were at this level. Ananias and Sapphira were deceived at this level.

I worked with one couple whose son's heart was like rock. He would rarely communicate with anyone outside his peer group, and then his communication was short and rude. Heavy metal music seemed to penetrate every cell of his brain, and he had decided that people who took God seriously were weird. His parents often didn't know where he went or what he did.

On top of this, his parents displayed throughout the house an array of idols they had collected while on vacation. They continually dealt with inexplicable depression and an endless string of illnesses. By this time in my life, I had learned my spiritual warfare lessons and was ready to intervene. But this couple was not willing to throw out the idols or to take a stand regarding their son or the devil. Their son did not change, and they did not get better.

Spiritual warfare can take place at what we might call the "cosmic level," when we confront powers of evil that influence groups, organizations, or places. Daniel 10 tells about the demonic powers over Persia and Greece; 1 and 2 Kings describe scads of Canaanite gods and goddesses that non-Israelite people worshiped; the Ephesus riot in Acts 19 may have been influenced at this level.

A cultic organization got a building permit to tear down a church and build their North American headquarters in our town—a temple the size of a football field. A few other intercessors and I fasted and prayed and asked God to dry up their money and thwart their plans. We prayed that a Christian church would reclaim the property. Their money did dry up but began to flow just before their building permit was set to expire. We kept praying. The city planning commission reversed its decision and denied an extension. The cultists vowed to appeal.

One day another intercessor and I marched around the property and prayed that the kingdom of God would be restored there. The property was on a hillside, and the Spirit seemed to tell me to pray Ezekiel 36. I had no clue what that chapter was until I read it: a prophecy to the mountains of Israel that God's people would be reestablished there.

While the other intercessor prayed in front of the building, I felt led to do the seven-lap Jericho march thing. On my second lap, as if Satan decided to show up, a rattlesnake slithered out from behind an electrical box, coiled, and hissed. Sometimes things happen in the physical realm that speak of realities in the spiritual realm. I knew in my gut I must not back away. I asked God's protection according to Psalm 91 and kept walking around, each time passing only a foot away from the hissing, rattling snake. My sixth time around it did something strange: it wriggled backward into the brush, facing me and hissing as it disappeared. For two years we kept praying and watching. And the cult put the property up for sale. Totally unknown to us, the Holy Spirit had been leading another church to pray for the property. After a string of financial miracles, they purchased it and now thrive there.

NOT POWER BUT OBEDIENCE

I discovered that spiritual warfare does not center on power. Power is not, and must not be, the issue. First of all, God is infinitely stronger than the enemy. Second, interest in power invariably leads to problems. I've seen people focus more on power than on Jesus, and they indulge in duking it out with the devil as if they were starring in an ESPN boxing match. We call on the power of God, yet God also says, "My power is made perfect in weakness" (2 Cor. 12:9). When we accept our own weaknesses, we will see more of God's power.

Our victory is based on authority. Authority is gained by our obedience. Imagine how foolish Joshua and his army must have felt traipsing around Jericho in silence once a day for six days, then seven times the seventh day. Imagine how crazy it might have seemed to Gideon, with 32,000 fighting men, to be told to reduce the number by more than 99 percent to a mere 300. Imagine how terrified Jehoshaphat's choir would have felt at being told to sing and march at the front of the army as they went into battle. When the Israelites obeyed God's law, they had victory every single time. When they turned away from God, they did nothing but lose.

The spiritual battles we face are not ours anyway. God makes this clear when he tells Jehoshaphat to face the enemy: "The battle is not yours, but God's" (2 Chron. 20:15). In the next verse God gives the job description for the human side of things: "Tomorrow march down against them" (v. 16). Simply put, it's *God's* battle, but *we* do the marching.

FOCUS ON JESUS

I know a pastor who focused so much on casting demons out of people that demon expulsion became the main event every Sunday morning. The demons must have had a great time getting all that attention. My guess is that they jumped around from person to person (or at least got people to think so) and stole the attention away from Jesus. Members started criticizing what was going on until the church split, and those who remained felt demoralized.

I learned a lesson: do not focus on the demonic; focus on Jesus. While it is important to know about the demonic, we're not in a boxing match. Our focus needs to be on Jesus. Demons should never be allowed to distract our attention from him. When we focus on our master, we can trust him to deal with the demonic.

SPIRITUAL WARFARE AS A LIFESTYLE

I have learned not to treat spiritual warfare as an activity by itself but as part of my overall Christian life. The Bible says, "Do everything in love" (1 Cor. 16:14). That's the best motivation for spiritual warfare. Love keeps us humble, on track with God, and motivated to help others. Prayer is love on its knees. A Christlike lifestyle is love in action. Love on its knees means we pray for people because we love them. Love in action means we actively care for people because we love them.

I have also learned not to underestimate the power of holiness. Holy-living people are dangerous to the devil. They tend not to fall into the devil's snares. On top of that, they lead others out of snares. It's hard for the devil to find a foothold in the lives of people who live under the lordship of Christ and love him with a pure heart. I'm not talking about self-satisfied personal piety, which is really not holiness at all. I'm talking about heart purity with a purpose: to serve God by loving him and loving others, to live free and help others find freedom from what binds them.

To experience spiritual victory rather than defeat, "let us throw off everything that hinders and the sin that so easily entangles" (Heb. 12:1). God wants us clean and whole. When we are, we will live free and help others to do the same.

PRAYER
~ *Starter* ~

Lord, I acknowledge that the battle I face is yours. And I commit to doing my part in whatever I must do. Lead me to walk by faith and exercise your authority in overcoming the evil I face. Surround and protect me as you've promised. . . .

MOVING
OUT

— DAY 26 —

PRAYER OF AGREEMENT

One of our family members, John, earned $1,500 a month as a sportscaster for a small radio station, and he needed a bigger income. His job required a lot of entertaining and parties, which involved rivers of alcohol and took him away from his family. Kim urged him to repent of the alcohol-saturated lifestyle and to work elsewhere. Following her lead, he repented and rejected the radio station's offer of a new position with a substantially higher salary. Instead he found a part-time position with a major telecommunications firm that agreed to fund his education, and six months later he went full-time at the new job—for a hundred dollars less per month than he had made at the radio station. He struggled to support his wife and child, with another baby on the way. He grew angry at Kim and told her,

"Because of your misguidance, my finances are ruined!" To add to the sting, his company had a policy: employees with a college degree in business administration or telecommunications made twice as much as those with a degree in economics, as he had.

Kim challenged him: "Do you believe in God's provision? Do you believe God will listen when we agree in faith according to his promise in Matthew 18:19–20, that when two of us agree in prayer, we will have what we ask for? God can change the company policy."

"No way," he said. "Don't kid yourself. That's not going to happen."

She ignored his words and went to his apartment to pray with him and his wife that night. They waited on God and sensed his leading to agree in faith that the company policy would change. They all prayed together until two a.m. Then they waited.

In less than a month, the company changed its policy. They would now give economics majors the same pay scale as business and telecommunications majors. The effective date was the day John's second child was born. And in addition to that, the company made the salary adjustment retroactive. So John received thousands of dollars in back pay. From that point he continually received promotions and raises.

THE FOUNDATION OF AGREEMENT

I wondered about this curious dynamic of agreement in prayer and grew convinced that it's not mechanical but personal. The foundation is relationship, and it starts with God. Ephesians 2 says that we were all spiritually dead and alienated from God, then made "alive with Christ" (v. 5). This means we were once separated from God, our source of life, then connected through Christ. We also enter our proper place in the spiritual world. Verse 6 says that we are "seated" with Christ "in the heavenly realms." That is, because of our relationship with Jesus, we have a high position of spiritual authority. It doesn't stop there. The rest of chapter 2 tells how getting right with God opens the way for reconciliation with other people. Together we are all "fellow citizens with God's people and members of God's household" (v. 19). Agreement in prayer centers on relationships: with God, with our position in the spiritual world, and with other people.

So when we agree with someone in prayer, we're doing a lot more than checking off the same item on our lists.

THE POWER OF AGREEMENT (BIBLICAL MATH)

Through their entire history, the Israelites have faced hostile neighbors. And God promised in Leviticus 26:8, "Five of you will chase a hundred, and a hundred of you will chase ten thousand." I did the math and found that going from five versus a hundred to a hundred versus ten thousand is a fivefold increase in impact. When the group increases twenty times (from five to a hundred), the effectiveness does not increase an equivalent twenty times; it increases a hundred times!

At the end of his career, Moses recalled a similar exponential increase when just two people came together: "How could one man chase a thousand or two put ten thousand to flight . . . unless the LORD had given them up?" (Deut. 32:30). This dynamic is more than effective teamwork or crowd psychology. It's spiritual. When people come together to confront the enemy, God works exponentially more than when they do it alone.

The point is not to use a calculator when praying with others. Rather it is to enter into the phenomenon of exponential increase when, by faith, we agree with God's leading and with other people of like mind.

Jesus applies this same principle to prayer in Matthew 18:19–20: "If two of you on earth agree about anything you ask for, it will be done for you by my Father in heaven. For where two or three come together in my name, there am I with them." This doesn't mean we should not pray alone. I do most of my praying alone. It seems that most leaders of the Bible did too. But this verse tells us that there are times when joining in prayer with others yields great results.

Jesus' promise here seems to have one stipulation. Verse 20 says, "Where two or three come together in my name, there am I with them." The phrase "come together" is better translated as "have been gathered"—as in, God has something to do with people's coming together and praying. So when God leads us to pray together and leads us how to pray, we can expect greater results than when we're doing our own thing.

Daniel Nash, whom we met earlier, understood this. Charles Finney's great nineteenth-century revivals rode on this man's fervent prayers. But the existing records show that Nash regularly had others join him in intercession. He and his friend Abel Clary spent days and weeks holed up together in apartments or basements, praying for revival. People don't do that unless God leads them. Nash knew the power of agreement.

AGREEMENT WITH GOD'S WORD AND SPIRIT

I've grown convinced that agreement in prayer doesn't start when we pray. It starts by agreeing with God and his Word. That includes what I think, what I say, and what I do or don't do. It starts with living in obedience to God's Word and in harmony with the Holy Spirit. So before I get serious in prayer, I check how aligned my life is with God. I haven't scored perfectly yet, but I find that God is gracious when my heart's attitude is right.

The Bible contains over seven thousand promises. (I never counted them, but other preachers apparently did.) And Jesus said, "Until heaven and earth disappear, not the smallest letter, not the least stroke of a pen, will by any means disappear" (Matt. 5:18). That tells me I've got a truckload of promises that Jesus is serious about fulfilling. So when I agree with God's Word, I have a lot of promises to choose from.

As we saw in day 9, the Holy Spirit leads us when we listen. When we follow, we agree with the Spirit by what we do and how we pray. If only it were always easy. Sometimes it is, and it can be great fun. But other times the Spirit leads us to do something we don't like, yet in the end we can see how it was the right way.

When God called me to leave Minnesota and go all the way to California for seminary, I resisted. It was too far and too expensive, and my mother needed someone to help her. I found myself lying on the floor, trembling and sensing God's voice drumming in my head, until I finally gave in and went. The plane ride took only three hours and twenty minutes. God provided for every financial need. And people never stopped helping my mother. I learned the value of agreeing with the Holy Spirit.

AGREEMENT WITH OTHERS

Once we agree with God's Word and Spirit, we can be in better accord with others, because we know what to agree on. It's important to find a point, even if it's not the ideal, where we can be of the same mind and faith as the ones with whom we pray. If each person believes for different things, we may as well pray by ourselves.

With John, whom I mentioned earlier, I learned the other side of agreeing in prayer. He commuted an hour and a half to work, and for months I prayed with him that the company would relocate him closer, so he could have more time with his family and the church. But nothing happened. When I asked him about it, he confessed that he had actually been happy enough with his job to endure the long commute and really didn't want to change. So in his heart he had actually been disagreeing with my prayer. Sheesh! No wonder my prayers had gone unanswered.

Hebrews 11:1 says that "faith is being sure of what we hope for." God never tells us to simply *hope* something comes true. He tells us to be sure of it. Agreement is the specific point at which we mutually place our expectation. Thankfully God answers prayer because he is compassionate, not because we earn it. Even if our faith is like a tiny mustard seed, God will work with it (Matt. 17:20).

When people have an illness or injury that requires hospital treatment or an operation, I always ask them what they will believe God for. I encourage them to stretch their faith, but I still pray for them at their faith level. Only then are we agreeing in prayer, and only then can we expect fulfillment of Jesus' promise in Matthew 18:19. Our conversation might go like this:

> "How do you want me to pray for you?" I ask.
>> "I just want God to bless me," the person responds.
>> "Can you be more specific?"
>> "Well, I just want to be healed."
>> "What exactly will you believe God for?"
>> "What do you mean?"
>> "Will you believe God for a total healing so you won't have to undergo surgery? Or will you believe God for a miraculously fast and complete recovery? Or will you believe God to guide the doctors and have a good recovery?"

People will concur at any of these three degrees of faith, and I've found that prayers of agreement commonly get answered at the levels where people put their faith.

Over the years I've also found both in the Bible and in life experience that the only times God does not require faith from people—and when they do not need to agree in prayer—is when they're small children, unconscious, or dead. Really. It seems that God expects a person making a request either to have faith or to agree with someone who does.

Some people stare at me when I ask if they'll believe for a miracle, so we end up praying for wisdom or an open door. Others will abandon themselves to God, and together we wrestle by faith to receive the impossible. It's not always simple, and it's not always quick, but Jesus did say, and meant, "according to your faith" (Matt. 9:29). Wherever that is, it's the point of agreement.

PRAYER
~ *Starter* ~

Lord, as I read your Word and seek the guidance
of your Spirit, lead me to pray in harmony with
your will. And as I pray with [name of person],
we agree in faith that you will do what you have
promised. . . .

SERVING THOSE
WE PRAY FOR

A middle school boy in our church liked to head butt other kids into the walls. One morning in Sunday school, he flipped the chair of a newcomer and gave the poor kid a bloody nose. The new family never came back. When I arranged for the aggressive boy to stay with his parents at all times for a month of Sundays, his mother informed me that I was the worst pastor she'd ever had. She didn't like the church board chairman either.

I prayed for the boy to change and for the mother to repent.

Our church maintained a commitment to help local families in need, whether they were part of our congregation or not. Our next big project was to help this very family. I prayed it would be called off. God didn't answer that one.

The Saturday morning we went to their house to fix their porch, I clenched my teeth to keep from saying anything nasty.

The church board chairman seemed to be clenching his teeth too. I found that I didn't say much when I served someone who didn't like me, and whom I didn't like either. If any of us had said much, we would only have caused trouble.

While we fixed the porch, I remembered something my mind must have misplaced: no matter what people think about me, or who they are, love them anyway. Love them in action, willfully. With every swing of the hammer, I felt how hard that can be. Sometimes I'd rather do anything but love people I don't like. But not loving them leaves both of us worse off. It drives us into swamps of self-justification, where unforgiveness poisons our souls, rots our relationships, and sabotages our health.

Every swamp has a path out—the way of love, acceptance, and forgiveness. The path is clearest and best traveled when it takes the form of actively loving people. We most actively love people when we serve them. The act of serving softens hardened attitudes—both for the one serving and for the one receiving. In a way, serving others saves us from ourselves, from the results of living in the swamp.

By the time I finished working on her porch, this woman had become respectful toward me, even kind. And I had let go of my self-righteous anger toward her. Two hardened hearts were redeemed through an act of kindness.

Serving Others

For most of us, willfully loving hard-to-love people is not natural or normal. We are short on that kind of love. We have to get it from God. The Bible calls that love *agape*—the word used to describe the love of God. It has nothing to do with romantic feelings or cozy "you love me and I love you" arrangements. *Agape* is a love that seeks out and does what is best for another person, even if that person is abusive or full of hate. Because *agape* comes from God, it invariably takes us beyond ourselves. It compels us to do things we would never do otherwise. Mother Teresa told of an Australian man who came and "made a substantial donation. But as he did this he said, 'This is something external. Now I want to give something of myself.' He now comes regularly to the house of the dying to shave the sick men and to converse with them."[1] *Agape.* God loves through us. We are his containers to love and serve a sometimes unlovable world.

Some of us serve a lot; some of us don't. I thought about what has kept me from serving—usually things like fear, self-centeredness, pride, lack of love, or just being oblivious. But if we're following our leader, we can't escape his example. Jesus took a towel and water basin and washed his disciples' feet. They were taken aback and didn't know how to respond. Jesus instructed them and kept washing. He finished and said, "I have set you an example that you should do as I have done for you. . . . Now that you know these things, you will be blessed if you do them" (John 13:15, 17). If the master is a servant, I'll take my place beside him. He even promises to bless me when I do.

The flip side of all this is to pray for those whom we already serve. We may serve people in our workplace, church, or family. Praying for them adds a spiritual dimension to tasks that may otherwise be mundane. And doing so will transform our whole attitude about a job.

THE ATTITUDE OF SERVING

Mother Teresa said, "Spend your time in prayer. If you pray you will have faith, and if you have faith, you will naturally want to serve."[2] Mother Teresa followed a history of people who prayed much and served the poor of their day: Francis of Assisi in thirteenth-century Italy, Catherine of Siena in fourteenth-century Italy, Catherine of Genoa in fifteenth-century Italy, Vincent de Paul in seventeenth-century France, and William Booth in nineteenth-century England. The ministries of these and many others rose out of prayer, and these people served the poor and the sick with passion, making every bit as much of an impact in their own day as Mother Teresa did in hers. Who among us will God raise up now?

However we serve, we still choose our attitude. Outward acts may look the same, but their motivations will vary. Servility says, "I have to"; servanthood says, "I want to." Servility serves without love; servanthood serves because of love. Servility lives by the approval of others; servanthood lives in harmony with God.

Dr. Paul Brand tells of Abbe Pierre, who organized beggars to help themselves and serve one another in Paris in the decades after World War II. The beggars did so well that Abbe Pierre came to a crisis point: they no longer had anyone worse off than themselves to serve! He knew his followers would become ingrown and self-serving. He had to find someone for his beggars to help. So he went to a leprosy hospital in Vellore, India, then returned to Paris and inspired his beggars to raise money to build a ward at the hospital. He expressed his view of service this way: "We must serve or we die."[3]

WHAT SERVING OTHERS DOES

I stand amazed at my growing list of benefits from serving others. Serving others breaks down bad feelings toward them. It's hard to maintain bitterness or criticism toward someone we're serving. Serving others replaces bad feelings with the attitude of Jesus.

Often when we begin serving others, we carry our own agenda of who they are and what they need. But the act of serving them enables us to see past appearances and past our assumptions of what they need, to who they really are and what they really need.

After serving people, we carry the memories with us. Those memories often motivate us to pray for those people more than if we hadn't served them.

More than anything else, serving others merges our prayer and our action. As I said in day 25, prayer is love on its knees. A Christlike lifestyle—in this case, serving others—is love in action. They are two sides of one coin, and each side enhances the other.

When we serve those we pray for, we often discover that we become part of the answer to our own prayer. Our actions take on a spiritual dimension—God is part of what we're doing, and he is working through us. Our actions can influence those we pray for so that they grow more receptive to receiving what God wants to do in their lives. Kim is always busy helping every church member and every person outside the church that God brings our way. It's no surprise that they open their hearts to God and experience many answers to her prayers.

How to Serve Others

It's often easier to love people who are far away than those who are near. Acts of service toward strangers or faraway people are sometimes easier because they are temporary (short-term mission trips last maybe one or two weeks) and less demanding (checks are often easier to give than labor). On the other hand, if we love those around us, we'll show it by serving. Every one of us has unique abilities, gifts, and ways to serve others.

Many times we have an innocent reason for not serving: it simply doesn't occur to us. We're busy, and the needs of others simply don't register on our overloaded mental control panels. Even when others don't have an obvious need, finding simple ways to bless them will often uplift them in the same way as meeting a need would.

That's why, unless we're grinches, the best thing we can do is alert ourselves ahead of time for opportunities to serve. Ask people how they are doing—and listen. We may be the only ones all day who do. And that's how doors open into people's lives.

We can easily compliment them, encourage them, or call them on their birthday. With a bit more effort, we could invite them for a meal, assist them financially, or care for them when they're sick. If we've got the time, we could give them a ride, help them with a project, or babysit their kids. If we've got the energy, we could make or fix something, rake their lawn, or help clean their house.

When we do these sorts of things, Jesus equates them to serving *him*, especially when we help the poor or the oppressed. He says, "Whatever you did for one of the least of these brothers of mine, you did for me" (Matt. 25:40). But he goes further and relates that to our going to heaven, essentially saying that those who serve get a heavenly inheritance with God, while those who don't get a fiery inheritance with the devil.

Wait, this Matthew 25 stuff seems to contradict all the salvation-by-faith verses. Or perhaps it's some kind of verification of who's really saved. I'd go with the second choice. Though we don't get to heaven by doing good works, Jesus seems to say here that the *genuineness* of our belief is revealed by *how we act*, that the things we deeply, truly believe are the ones we live out. Serving others for the sake of Jesus ranks high on the list of ways to live out our faith.

Service to those we pray for does not have to be worthy of a newspaper article. It can be small. Brother Lawrence said, "We ought never weary of doing little things for the love of God, who really doesn't think about the greatness of what we do but the love with which we do it."[4] In big ways or small, love serves others.

As you serve those you pray for, you will probably see the dynamic mirrored: you will pray more for those you serve.

PRAYER
~ Starter ~

> Lord, open my eyes to see the ways in which I
> can serve the people for whom I pray. As I help
> others, may they and I experience the power of
> your love. . . .

WRITING IT DOWN

Two men sat by a fire on the Mount of Olives and gazed across the Kidron Valley. Throughout the rolling hills of Jerusalem, flickering flames punctuated the night sky with gentle warmth.

"I think we should write the stories down," Mark said.

Peter stretched his hands toward the fire. "Why? I was with Jesus for three years, and every believer around here knows the stories. Besides, people sit around these fires at night and remember everything word for word." A knotted branch crackled and settled on the embers. "Most people don't know how to read anyway. You know that."

"Something still tells me to write it down." Mark stood and paced in a circle. "I know I messed up when I was young, and Paul wouldn't take me on his second trip. But thanks to Barnabas

I've changed. And when I reconnected with Paul, I saw how he and his guys write down everything the churches need to hear." He stopped and spread his arms. "It's amazing. People carry his letters all over the Roman Empire. People he's never even met are changed."

"So I've heard." Peter tossed a stick on the fire. "Are you sure? It's a lot to tell—miracles, parables, teaching. We'd have to include the conflicts with the Pharisees. The crucifixion. The resurrection."

"You're not going to live forever, Peter. I'll write it all down for you. And years from now, if Jesus doesn't return by then, the church will still have his story."

"The gospel. In written form." Peter stared at the flames as if absorbed in them. "Yes, let's do it."

KEEPING A RECORD

We don't know how the conversation really went. But we do know that the biblical writers did not want the testimony of what God said and did in the world to be forgotten.

Ancient scribes had limited options. Chiseling into stone was like, well, chiseling into stone. Parchment, which was made from the skins of sheep or goats, was expensive. And papyrus, which was made from river reeds pasted together, was bumpy. But they wrote anyway, because the message was important. Now we laser words onto paper at pennies a sheet and tap on electronic gizmos that upgrade every few months. The folks from back then would be jealous.

Throughout history, Christian devotional classics developed from the written records of people's encounters with God. Augustine's *Confessions* reads like a long prayer journal. John of the Cross's *Dark Night of the Soul* is a passionate love poem with commentary. Julian of Norwich's *Revelations of Divine Love* is a record of visions she received.

God still communicates and works in our lives today. I realized early on that if I didn't write things down, much of what God said or did in my life would be lost in the dusty backlogs of fading memories.

ANSWERS TO PRAYER

Nothing encourages us to pray like answers to previous prayers. We could study and sing all day about why we should pray, but if we review a list of our own answered prayers, we can't help but want to pray more.

When I am discouraged or just lethargic, I sometimes look back to notes of prayer God has answered: zero debt when I graduated from two graduate programs, Kim's healing from a cancerous tumor, my daughter's recovery from childhood emotional damage, God's leading on major life decisions . . . and smaller prayers too, like finding a parking space. Even the times I didn't get what I had asked, I still got what I needed. Yet I so easily lose sight of how many times God has answered, and I see that in other people too. We all forget the collective impact of answered prayers.

Aimee Semple McPherson, an early nineteenth-century evangelist and founder of the Foursquare Church, went beyond writing things down. In her home church, Angelus Temple, she displayed crutches and wheelchairs of people who were healed. To this day they have stood as testimonies of God's healing power and have inspired worshipers to boldly continue seeking God. Whenever I look at my decades-long list of answered prayers, I remember: if the Lord did it then, he will do it again.

MENTAL IMPRESSIONS

If we're attentive when we pray, at some point we'll sense some kind of mental impression. If it's not our own drifting thoughts, it might be the Holy Spirit speaking to us. Writing down the impression is the first step toward figuring out what to do with it and maybe putting it into action.

Jesus says that the Holy Spirit "will teach you all things and will remind you of everything I have said to you" (John 14:26). Also, "He will guide you into all truth . . . by taking from what is mine and making it known to you" (16:13–14). We should *expect* God to communicate with us. He clearly intends to. When we write things down, we're being good stewards of his communication.

Most of my best ideas come from other people or from God. I'm sure of it. I've learned to listen for God's voice, meditate on Scripture, and write down significant thoughts when they come—maybe a new insight, someone to pray for, or something I need to change. Whatever the source, if it's worth remembering, it's worth writing down.

Prophecies

Prophecy literally means "to speak for," as in, someone speaks for God. The Bible says, "Do not treat prophecies with contempt. Test everything. Hold on to the good" (1 Thess. 5:20–21). Treating prophecies with contempt means not only to disregard them but also to forget about them. I doubt that God speaks in order for us to ignore or forget what he says. Whether a prophecy comes through someone with a prophetic gift or through powerful preaching, it should be tested. Testing takes time and works a lot better if we've written down the prophecy.

I don't receive a lot of prophecies, but when I do, I try to write them down as soon as possible. Seeing the words on paper helps me pray about them over time, test them, and figure out whether they're really from God or just someone's idea. If they seem legit, I agree with God about them, pray, and watch what happens.

If you're skeptical about prophecies given today, writing them down is a great way to track them and discover whether what you hear is valid.

Journaling

Keeping a prayer journal is a way of praying on paper. Some find journaling helpful both to record and to stimulate their prayers. Writing out prayers is a bit like vocalizing them, only more clearly thought out. The two main ingredients of a prayer journal are prayers to God and God's answers. Prayer journals can also include thoughts and observations, insights from

Scripture, and things the Lord tells us. These things make a prayer journal a good tool for self-examination, whether for confession of sin or reflection on where we are in life.

Keeping a journal of our spiritual journey is another option. This can be done daily as a diary or as an occasional milepost record of what we're going through. I do the milepost option and find it a great way to see how God has worked in my life—which helps me make better sense of my life right now. Without journal entries, many of my experiences would drift into fuzzy "back then something happened" recollections. Looking back at these entries is not only fun, but it also sets a helpful pattern for my future direction.

Journaling is not for everyone. If you find it too tedious, you're in luck—Scripture does not command journal keeping.

Keeping Notes

We all write things down differently, right? For example, those of us who thrive on chaos may keep a hodgepodge of notes on church bulletins, napkins, and envelopes. The more organized among us may systematize neatly written pages in a three-ring binder, where pages can be added, classified, or removed. The electronically inclined may use a PDA or computer to keep a database. The artistically inclined may weave everything together into beautifully bound books of blank pages and marbled covers.

How much to write is up to you. Elite stenographers will probably keep reams of notes. Most people like me just jot down the most important words. We all have at least one answered prayer or something God has communicated to us. What's yours?

PRAYER
~ Starter ~

Lord, as I review insights, past answers to prayer, and things I've heard from you, inspire me to pray more—and with greater faith. You did it then; you'll do it again. . . .

— *DAY 29* —

RAISING VOICES TOGETHER

In May 1940 the Nazis stood on the verge of an all-out victory in Europe. They had trapped 400,000 British and French troops between the cliffs and the sea at Dunkirk on France's north coast. If those troops were killed or captured, Britain would fall to Nazi invasion. The European theater of World War II would be over before the United States even entered it.

But God raised a man to stand in the gap. Rees Howells, an intercessor and the founder of the Bible College of Wales, organized nightly intercessory prayer meetings with his students. From the battle of Dunkirk "through all the years of the war the whole College was in prayer every evening from seven o'clock to midnight with only a brief interval for supper. They never missed a day. This was in addition to an hour's prayer meeting every morning and very often at midday."[1] Morning, noon, and night, all through the war, they never missed a night. Howells said to his intercessors: "God will not do a bit more through you than you have faith for. . . . You are more responsible for this victory today than those men on the battlefield." He added, "I feel tonight that whatever the Nazis do, they cannot escape the Holy Spirit."[2] Parliament also called for a national day of prayer on May 26.

Instead of wiping out the troops as he could have, Hitler held his army back, content to bomb Dunkirk day after day from a distance. During that time, ships, yachts, and even rowboats evacuated 338,000 troops across the English Channel—as the water remained miraculously calm. Hitler's behavior was inexplicable, except in that God held him back in response to the prayers of believers. Howells's group poured their hearts out to God for hours every day, and the whole nation joined in. It seemed the Lord couldn't say no.

Only four months later, in September 1940, the Battle of Britain found the German Luftwaffe devouring Britain's outnumbered Royal Air Force. Great Britain floundered on the brink of Nazi invasion. Even more than at Dunkirk, Hitler stood poised to rule all of Europe. Hope seemed lost, but not to Rees Howells and his students. After Howells sought the Holy Spirit's leading, it was said of him that "faith would stand to the claim and lay hold of the victory; and there would be no rest until he had God's own assurance that faith had prevailed and victory was certain."[3] The British suffered to the point of certain defeat, when suddenly radar screens showed the German planes moving east. Minutes later, the fighting ended as the Luftwaffe, with a sure victory in hand, let it go and turned home. There is no earthly explanation for why Hitler called off the fight. But the heavenly explanation is clear.

I do not believe I overstate when I say Rees Howells and his students deserve great credit for Britain being saved and thus turning the tide of the whole European war.

Wouldn't you love to pray in a group that changes lives and the world around us? You may not change the course of a world war, but you can surely change the course of a person or a family, a church or a community.

ORGANIZED PRAYER GROUPS

Most groups go through ups and downs, plateaus and break-throughs. I started a prayer group that took four years to reach a healthy dynamic—then it fizzled when the church transitioned. But now we have new groups. For every group that ends, a new one begins. Through much trial and error, I've discovered a few things that help a prayer group keep its focus and vitality. If you're involved in one, you might consider some of these things.

Take charge. A meeting without a person to lead or facilitate it often wanders off into lots of talk and little prayer. A facilitator makes sure the meeting stays focused. The meeting may include a brief Bible study, prayer requests, and regular prayer topics. Whether the leader is official or not, or whether the same person leads every time, is secondary. Occasionally a person may need to dump their feelings and talk for a while. That's fine, but most of the time your group will be glad to keep on track for the reason they gather.

Get close. Lots of empty space, especially around large tables, creates a feeling of separateness. That will weaken a group's dynamic. Sitting together in a close circle increases people's sense of togetherness, which enhances the overall prayer dynamic.

Skip the food. It's hard to seek God's face while we're stuffing ours. Food and drinks relax us and help us talk more—but they don't help us pray. They are fine at a table separate from the prayer circle and preferably should be finished or set aside before prayer. Consider serving refreshments after the meeting, when folks can socialize as long as they like.

Share the prayer. When one person prays long, others tend to mentally drift or lose interest. I sure do; don't you? Shorter prayers build better group dynamics because all members of the group pray more frequently—similar to having a conversation. I sometimes remind prayer group leaders that their main job is to encourage others to pray.

The bottom line is that the meeting format is less important than connecting with God. I'm less concerned with the program and more concerned with the Holy Spirit's leading. That's why I open group prayer with a focus on honoring God and inviting the Spirit to lead.

GROUPS THAT DON'T MEET PHYSICALLY

Even if you live on the Alaskan tundra, you can join a group that doesn't meet physically. Thanks to satellites, telephones, and email, people scattered over endless miles can form groups that unite in prayer—just not in the same location. They will agree on a single issue, at the same time if they like. Of course these groups don't have the same dynamics as groups that meet together, but for some of us they're a good choice. And they often connect to local groups that meet face-to-face.

My evangelist friend Elaine Pettit coordinates an army of more than two thousand people across the country who daily pray for her ministry and for local churches, with email updates every week. Some of her pray-ers meet at churches and in homes, particularly in the weeks preceding a scheduled revival meeting. But whether their contact is virtual or in person, they bond together in purpose. The results show: large numbers of people come to faith, lives transform, and folks get healed and have even risen from the throes of death. Individuals who link up with groups like this are no different from anyone else. They just like to pray. If you have a friend or two who wants to form a prayer network, no distance can stop you.

A FAMILY AFFAIR

In 2 Timothy 1:5 Paul acknowledges Timothy's "sincere faith," which he said "first lived in your grandmother Lois and in your mother Eunice and, I am persuaded, now lives in you also." We don't know how Timothy's grandmother and mother passed their faith on to him. But something was going on in that family—they spent time together with God in the center.

A common, traditional approach to family spirituality is

"family devotions," in which a family reads the Bible or a Bible lesson and prays together. Bruce Wilkinson, who has devoted his life to helping Christians read and apply the Bible more effectively, finds that most Christian families don't do family devotions—and they feel guilty about it. Yet most who grew up in homes that did them have negative recollections: boring, oppressive, and irrelevant.[4]

Wilkinson says that to be effective, family devotions must be a regularly scheduled activity, adding that "you'll make time for what is important to you."[5] Most families won't be able to do them every day but should be able to at least once a week. After supper or before bed are the most common times. He also says that this time should not be a Bible study or a sermon but interaction on a biblically oriented subject that is meaningful to those participating. If the ages of the children are too far apart, do devotions separately with younger and older kids. Doing devotions also takes practice—don't quit if it doesn't work the first or second time.[6]

On the other hand, Richard Foster makes me feel better when he discusses the low numbers of families doing devotions:

> [The low numbers] represent a change in cultural patterns more than a lack of piety in the family. When farming communities and large families were predominant and gathering for meals and evening activities was common, this kind of family altar made perfect sense. For most of us, however, those days are gone. We live in urban surroundings and belong to small families. We eat out at fast-food restaurants much of the time and have to contend with ballet lessons and basketball practice and PTA meetings all in the same evening.[7]

My guilt is relieved. Still, I'd hate if we declared defeat due to the hyperactivity that has spread like a computer virus through most of our lives. Some of us may still be able to do family devotions the traditional way. Most of us can probably find new ways that will work.

I've learned to let spiritual issues out of the church and into my daily life. When Jesus is a natural part of my life, I naturally talk about him and behave like his follower. Spontaneous interaction and prayer with others is the kind of life and group involvement that most genuinely conveys my faith to others, and others' faith to me. My experience with my daughter is that when faith and prayer are part of my daily life—and hers— she responds more positively and embraces faith, prayer, and a Christian lifestyle more than if I did the God stuff only at designated times. It's the fruit of a genuine commitment and lifestyle.

If you are single, you may have roommates, housemates, neighbors, or colleagues at work or school with whom you could regularly interact and pray. While family interaction strengthens existing family ties, interaction with other singles creates deeper friendship and spiritual ties with others who normally might not be tied to us at all. Either way, praying together enriches relationships.

LIMITLESS POSSIBILITIES

The possibilities for prayer groups are limitless. There was once a prayer group of diverse people whom the Holy Spirit unified into a big, spiritual family. In the early 1700s Moravian refugees escaping religious persecution in eastern Europe came to Count Nicholas von Zinzendorf's estate in Germany. They called it *Herrnhut*, "The Lord's Watch." The motley group nearly splintered from conflict and division, but a Holy Spirit revival drew them into unity. They began a twenty-four-hour-a-day prayer vigil, taking turns each hour. Out of that they sent missionary teams to twenty-eight countries in twenty-eight years, more than what all Protestants combined had sent out in the previous two centuries. At the center of their incredible achievement is something even more incredible: their prayer vigil continued around the clock, without interruption, for over one hundred years.[8] Imagine an unending prayer group that lasts longer than your entire life. Since they were the only ones in history to do that vigil, they're probably better seen as an inspiration than a comparison. If you're in a prayer group, what are your possibilities?

PRAYER
~ *Starter* ~

Lord, as we have gathered to pray as one, we honor you as master of the universe and of our lives. Holy Spirit, guide us as we pray. . . .

— *DAY 30* —

MAXIMUM EXPOSURE

Soon after I got serious about following Jesus, I realized that a lot of Christians I knew lived milquetoast spiritual lives—nice but dull, with little of the presence and power of God that I saw all over Scripture. As I hung around Kim and a few other "Spirit-filled" people, as they called themselves, I was sometimes shocked and often reoriented toward new ways of thinking. So I made this covenant: "Lord, I want all you have for me. If something is of you, I want it. Give me the discernment to know whether it is or not."

From that point on, I determined to expose myself to the whole spectrum of Christianity—from incense-burning priests to analytical scholars to people sprawled across the floor under the power of the Holy Spirit. God always seemed kind enough to give me discernment as to what I should and shouldn't buy into. Some things I did not like. But that was all part of my covenant—stepping past comfort zones to experience more of God. A few friends thought I was crazy. But I suspect I'd have been a fool to draw boundaries around my safe spiritual experiences and deprive myself of everything else God had for me.

From the time I met Kim, I went with her to Korean prayer meetings. These folks shouted. They swayed, sweated, and swooned. Whenever I figured I'd prayed enough, Kim would tell me, "Pray more." I could hardly hear her over the shouting. And I repeatedly asked, "Why do they shout? Why don't they sit still? Why do they pray so long?" Eventually I recognized—and appreciated—their intensity and passion.

On the opposite side of the spectrum, Russian Orthodox believers, who are formal and quiet, connect with the mystical presence of God through their candles and prayer. For them God is wrapped in mystery, and their icons speak not to logic but to intuition. I discovered a different way of connecting with God.

Just when I thought I was good at exploring what God had for me, along came a friend of mine, whom I'll call Mike. Though he was a believer, the results of unhealed pain (among other things) in his earlier life were dragging his marriage, his career, and his whole life into a pit. He told me, "My life was completely broken. It was life and death. I was emotionally broken from my childhood, from all of my father's verbal and physical abuse. He was an anti-father. My home was a war zone."

As time went on, I watched Mike change and grow. First he climbed out of the pit onto stable ground. Now he has grown into an international Christian leader, and he partners with other ministries to make a significant impact for Jesus Christ across the region in which he lives. I pieced together how he did this. First out of desperation, then out of hunger for God, Mike read and listened to everything he could from well-known Christian leaders. He reviewed, internalized, even prayed over what he learned. Then he got me to read and listen too—and my boundaries were stretched until I nearly ripped.

I found that when I reached beyond myself, I grew beyond fear of the unknown and habits of the known. I grew into a bigger person spiritually—toward the size God intended. As I reached, I found that in order to try new things without criticizing them, I needed humility. And to keep from being duped, I needed discernment.

That's why I exercise what I call "skeptical open-mindedness." If I explore unfamiliar teaching or experiences with open-mindedness tempered by a pinch of healthy skepticism, I benefit every time. I look into things I wouldn't otherwise consider, yet I'm careful not to be gullible. I highly recommend that. I've exposed myself to a lot of things that have caused the straight-laced evangelical in me to cry, "That can't be of God!" (Translation: "That's different from what I'm used to!") Some experiences and teachings do turn out to be off base. Others are mixed, with a valuable lesson buried in the middle. Everything must pass the sniff test: is it compatible with the Bible?

A parable of a father who had three sons expresses the discernment I'm talking about. To test his sons' wisdom, the man gave each son an apple with a worm in it. The first son said, "An apple! Who cares if it has a worm in it?" He ate the whole thing and got sick. The second son said, "A worm! I won't eat that!"

He threw the whole thing away and went hungry. The third son said, "An apple with a worm!" He cut the worm out and ate the rest of the apple. He was the wisest.

I encourage you to join me and step beyond your comfort zones. In most cases God does not respect them nearly as much as we do. I'm not telling you to leave your church tradition, but read, attend, or do things you're not used to. You'll eventually find that it's hard to shrink back to your original dimensions. You may not want to.

Let's look at three areas where new experiences can enrich our prayer lives.

SCRIPTURE

The Bible is full of passages that, if we take them seriously, will not only inspire us but will also change our prayer lives. Rather than write out all the passages, I'll let you look them up if they catch your interest.

Revelation 4. Do you ever feel like your prayers bounce back from the ceiling? Visualize this awe-inspiring revelation of the throne room of God. Getting this picture in mind when we pray may encourage and motivate like nothing else.

Revelation 5:8; 8:3–5. Around the world, incense symbolizes prayer. Scripture is no different (Ps. 141:2). Our prayers accumulate like incense in God's throne room until he hurls back fire from the censer in a depiction of answered prayer.

Psalms. The Psalms reveal amazing honesty. The psalmists poured out gripes and laments as readily as they poured out praise. They openly laid their issues before God, and as a result, their hearts calmed, their faith rose, and their hopes revived.

Genesis 32:22–30. Jacob wrestled with an angel and said, "I will not let you go unless you bless me" (v. 26). That's tenacity. When we pray with tenacity, not quitting until we get God's blessing, it changes not only our prayers but our whole lives.

Luke 22:39–46. Jesus prayed so intensely in Gethsemane that blood cells burst through his capillaries and seeped through his sweat glands. No one has ever prayed more intensely. Too many of us get drowsy when we pray—after all, our eyes are usually shut. Most of our prayers could use more intensity.

Colossians 4:12. When we love someone as much as Epaphras did, to wrestle (literally, "agonize") in prayer for him or her, our entire prayer lives are infused with adrenaline. Love is the best motivator for nearly anything.

OTHER PRACTICES OR GATHERINGS

Change and growth sometimes involve getting out the door. One place to go is a private prayer retreat for several days, or even for just a day. Many people fast during a prayer retreat. I take my Bible, a notebook, and sometimes inspirational books. It is an ideal place and time to practice topics in this book. If I'm gone for several days, I'll stay at a retreat center run by a church or parachurch organization. Monasteries and convents often rent rooms. And most Christian camps rent to individuals on weekdays.

Another trip out the door may lead to a prayer retreat with your local church or a prayer conference. People often experience breakthroughs at meetings like these. Along with the speakers, there will be time for group prayer, private prayer, and sometimes good food. Prayer ministries and church or neighborhood prayer groups may be even better because they meet consistently. Prayer groups are everywhere; we just have to find them—or start our own.

LIVES OF PRAYING PEOPLE

Paul wrote, "Follow my example, as I follow the example of Christ" (1 Cor. 11:1). We have living examples all around us. Trust me, you'll recognize them. Often they're senior citizens. Or they run a church prayer group. They're people who are quick to pray, who personally know the one they're praying to, and who expect results. They're serious because they recognize that all around us heaven and hell hang in the balance; yet they're joyful because they know that Jesus is our hope. Hang out and pray with them. Absorb their intimacy and passion.

Others have walked before us through history and have left incredible legacies. You've read about some in this book. Christian bookstores and libraries stock some of their stories, and the Internet overflows with them all. Here is a brief list of praying people who have left powerful examples and writings for our benefit: Augustine, Celtic Christians, Francis of Assisi, Gregory Palamas, Catherine of Siena, Thomas à Kempis, Catherine of Genoa, Teresa of Avila, John of the Cross, Brother Lawrence, Jeanne Guyon, the Moravians, David Brainerd, George Müller, E. M. Bounds, John Hyde, Rees Howells, Andrew Murray, Sadhu

Sundar Singh, Wang Ming-Dao, and Cho Yong-gi. I've learned not to compare myself to these spiritual giants, because I feel small by comparison. Rather I let them inspire and motivate me.

As you connect with God, may your heart grow and contain God's gift of himself.

PRAYER
~ *Starter* ~

Lord, expand my horizons, take me past my comfort zones, and lead me to experience all that you have for me. If something is of you, I want it. Give me the discernment to know if it is. . . .

Growth Gauges and Suggested Activities

Assess yourself in any of the topics covered throughout the book. Under each heading you will find two statements. Beneath each statement is a scale of 1 to 10—1 being "never or almost never" and 10 being "always or almost always." These are not intended to judge you but to help you see where you may be strong and where you may want to grow.

Below each pair of gauges you will find two suggested activities for personal growth in those same areas. Be blessed as you grow.

DAY 1: HUNGER FOR GOD

I can genuinely say that I'm hungry for God.

1   2   3   4   5   6   7   8   9   10

I want to experience the presence of God more than anything else in life.

1   2   3   4   5   6   7   8   9   10

- Identify an issue in your life through which your hunger for God could grow. Then pray, *Lord, increase my hunger for you through this.*
- Meditate on Bible verses that speak of eternity. Compare them with what *seems* important in this life.

DAY 2: INTIMACY WITH GOD

I am willing to pay the price to have intimacy with God.

1   2   3   4   5   6   7   8   9   10

I have an intimate relationship with God.

1   2   3   4   5   6   7   8   9   10

- Think of and talk to God as your Father, your dad in heaven. Do this consistently.
- Admit one thing in your life that prevents you from being more intimate with God, and deal with it.

DAY 3: HOLY PASSION

Others consider me to be passionate in my love and service for God.

1   2   3   4   5   6   7   8   9   10

I have a simple lifestyle that frees me to give passionate attention to God.

1   2   3   4   5   6   7   8   9   10

- Determine one way in which you can simplify your life, then do it. Consider the decrease in clutter a door to more intimacy with God.

- Identify one area of your life in which you will step out of your comfort zone and trust God. Give it a long-term try.

DAY 4: STARTING A DEAD ENGINE

When I have difficulty praying, I use an effective method to stimulate my prayer.

| 1 | 2 | 3 | 4 | 5 | 6 | 7 | 8 | 9 | 10 |

I vary my methods to stimulate prayer.

| 1 | 2 | 3 | 4 | 5 | 6 | 7 | 8 | 9 | 10 |

- Choose a written prayer and pray it as if it were your own words from your heart.
- Play an instrument or some recorded music while you pray. Allow the music to carry you into a sense of God's presence.

DAY 5: GETTING A FAITH LIFT

I am growing spiritually through my struggles of faith.

| 1 | 2 | 3 | 4 | 5 | 6 | 7 | 8 | 9 | 10 |

I try to pray according to God's will, and I have strong faith when I pray.

| 1 | 2 | 3 | 4 | 5 | 6 | 7 | 8 | 9 | 10 |

- Make a list of answered prayers that you or others have experienced. Review the list to help you trust God for a present need.
- Apply a Scripture verse to a prayer need, and beyond all doubt, willfully believe that God will do what he promises in his Word.

DAY 6: CLEANING HOUSE

I regularly confess my sins and make sure my relationship with God is right.

| 1 | 2 | 3 | 4 | 5 | 6 | 7 | 8 | 9 | 10 |

I regularly forgive and make sure my relationships with others are right.

| 1 | 2 | 3 | 4 | 5 | 6 | 7 | 8 | 9 | 10 |

- Name a sin, especially a hidden sin, of which you need to repent—then repent.

- If there's someone in your life whom you need to forgive, do whatever it takes to forgive that person.

DAY 7: CHARACTER GROWTH

In hard times, I go beyond asking God for help and invite him into my trouble.

1   2   3   4   5   6   7   8   9   10

My prayer includes confession, praise, thanksgiving, and meditation.

1   2   3   4   5   6   7   8   9   10

- Describe a hardship in your life, and seek God for how he might grow your character through it.

- Using the ACTS acronym (Adoration, Confession, Thanksgiving, and Supplication), estimate what proportion of time you spend in each of the four areas. You may want to increase the proportions of the first three.

DAY 8: PRAISE POWER

Praising God is a normal part of my prayer life.

1   2   3   4   5   6   7   8   9   10

I genuinely enjoy my prayer time and don't like to miss it.

1   2   3   4   5   6   7   8   9   10

- Deliberately praise God until you can honestly say he is lifting your heart and mind to a higher level.

- Express a need you have, and by faith praise God as the one who meets that need.

DAY 9: SPIRIT LED

When I pray, I sense promptings that seem to be from the Holy Spirit.

1   2   3   4   5   6   7   8   9   10

I yield the direction and content of my prayer to the Holy Spirit's leading.

1   2   3   4   5   6   7   8   9   10

- The next time you think the Holy Spirit may be leading you, give him the benefit of the doubt and follow. Assess the results.

- In prayer, clearly ask the Holy Spirit to lead you, expect him to lead you, and follow.

DAY 10: PRACTICING GOD'S PRESENCE

I am aware of God's presence in all the things I do throughout the day.

1   2   3   4   5   6   7   8   9   10

I deliberately set apart space in my heart for God throughout the day.

1   2   3   4   5   6   7   8   9   10

- Practice saying breath prayers like the Jesus Prayer or a spontaneous prayer. Evaluate how this changes your attitude on a busy day.

- In the midst of busyness or stress, stop everything for a few minutes and quietly think about God's presence with you.

DAY 11: A TIME TO LISTEN

Besides talking to God, I give time to quiet, meditative listening.

1   2   3   4   5   6   7   8   9   10

When I pray I receive and test what I think are leadings from the Holy Spirit.

1   2   3   4   5   6   7   8   9   10

- Sit quietly for five minutes and listen for what God might communicate to you.

- Read a chapter of the Bible—slowly, with a mind willing to engage with a verse that might jump out at you.

DAY 12: LIFTED VOICE

I voice my prayers out loud.

1   2   3   4   5   6   7   8   9   10

I clearly express my prayers.

1   2   3   4   5   6   7   8   9   10

- If you rarely or never pray out loud, go to a secluded place and speak quietly to God without worrying how it will sound.
- If you do pray out loud, raise your voice and release your emotions as you pray.

DAY 13: SPECIFICALLY SPEAKING

I pray specifically and put my faith on the line when expecting answers.

1   2   3   4   5   6   7   8   9   10

I seek God in what to pray and make specific requests.

1   2   3   4   5   6   7   8   9   10

- Identify one thing you have prayed about vaguely and turn it into a specific request.
- Ask God's leading regarding a prayer request and pray for that request as specifically as possible.

DAY 14: PRAYING GOD'S WORD

I regularly quote, personalize, or paraphrase Scripture in my prayer.

1   2   3   4   5   6   7   8   9   10

I confidently expect that God will do what he says in his Word.

1   2   3   4   5   6   7   8   9   10

- Read verbatim, paraphrase, or personalize a passage of Scripture as you pray, and incorporate that Scripture as part of your prayer.
- Choose a Bible verse and apply it to a specific situation, expecting God to do what his Word says.

DAY 15: THE EMPTY-STOMACH EFFECT

Fasting is a regular part of my prayer life.

1   2   3   4   5   6   7   8   9   10

When fasting, I experience intimacy with God and breakthrough in prayer.

1   2   3   4   5   6   7   8   9   10

- Fast in a way you never have before. Assess the influence it has on your spiritual life.

- If you are physically able, increase the amount of time you fast. Increase your amount of prayer along with the fasting.

DAY 16: ROOM RESERVATIONS

I have a designated place to pray that helps me focus on God.

1   2   3   4   5   6   7   8   9   10

I consistently (with occasional breaks) use my designated place to pray.

1   2   3   4   5   6   7   8   9   10

- Establish a place that to you is a personal sanctuary, a place that helps you naturally focus on God.

- Identify any common location and adapt how you normally use it to how you could use it for prayer.

DAY 17: SPECIAL APPOINTMENTS

I spend time with God as early as possible every day.

1   2   3   4   5   6   7   8   9   10

I consistently establish boundaries of prayer time.

1   2   3   4   5   6   7   8   9   10

- Set a specific time early each day that you will meet with God. Write it in your calendar if necessary.

- Practice intentional neglect regarding specific intruders on your time with God, such as phone calls, cleaning, work, study, or even people.

DAY 18: LIFTED HANDS AND FEET

I raise my hands when I pray, and my heart and mind are focused heaven-ward.

1   2   3   4   5   6   7   8   9   10

I move my body when I pray, and my prayer is generally more energized.

1   2   3   4   5   6   7   8   9   10

- Describe your typical posture when you pray. Change one aspect of your posture to express body language that is open to God.

- Walk while you pray. Find a secluded place large enough to move around in as you talk to God.

DAY 19: GUIDES OR NO GUIDES

I have identified how I pray best, with or without guides or lists.

1   2   3   4   5   6   7   8   9   10

I have put together and use a prayer guide that works well for me.

1   2   3   4   5   6   7   8   9   10

- Pray spontaneously but with a clear mental picture of the situation or Bible verse you're praying about.

- Compile a prayer guide using the suggestions in day 19.

DAY 20: MINIMIZING DISTRACTIONS

I pray in a place that offers few distractions.

1   2   3   4   5   6   7   8   9   10

I deal with distractions by writing notes or turning them into prayer topics.

1   2   3   4   5   6   7   8   9   10

- Look carefully at the place or places you pray. Remove or change anything that frequently distracts.

- If your mind wanders, commit to one of the suggested strategies to keep focused.

DAY 21: UNANSWERED PRAYER

I openly express my doubts to the Lord and allow him to lift me up.

1   2   3   4   5   6   7   8   9   10

When my prayers seem unanswered, I look for and often find reasons why.

1   2   3   4   5   6   7   8   9   10

- Consider an unanswered prayer in your life. Examine the reasons given in day 21 and decide if any of them apply to you.
- Think and pray about how you might deal with unanswered prayer. Determine your response ahead of time so that if it happens, you'll be ready.

DAY 22: THE WRESTLING RING

I wrestle in prayer with the tenacity not to let go until the issue is resolved.

1   2   3   4   5   6   7   8   9   10

I know I must "lose" to God in order to win, and I'm willing to do it.

1   2   3   4   5   6   7   8   9   10

- Identify something you wrestle—or could wrestle—with God about. Allow yourself to do that without feeling guilty.
- Apply 1 John 5:14–15 to what you wrestle about. Find a point of resolution, where you "lose" to God—then see how he blesses you.

DAY 23: SPRINTS AND MARATHONS

When I see an opportunity to pray on the spot, I seize the chance.

1   2   3   4   5   6   7   8   9   10

When my prayers seem to go unanswered, I keep praying anyway.

1   2   3   4   5   6   7   8   9   10

- Train yourself to pray for needs as you see them arise. To do this, mentally rehearse possible scenarios and how you will respond.
- Commit yourself to one prayer request for which you'll never give up praying.

DAY 24: PERSISTENT BOLDNESS

Whenever it's appropriate, I pray boldly.

1   2   3   4   5   6   7   8   9   10

I pray with expectation.

1   2   3   4   5   6   7   8   9   10

- Reconsider one prayer request you may have given up on and resolve to be persistent about it.

- Review one prayer request you have and raise your expectation in some measurable way.

DAY 25: THE GREAT WAR

I know my authority in Christ and renounce everything that ensnares me.

1   2   3   4   5   6   7   8   9   10

I generally recognize and resist the devil's schemes.

1   2   3   4   5   6   7   8   9   10

- Identify a situation in your life or someone else's that may involve demonic spiritual activity. Relate a Scripture verse to it, and let the verse guide you in prayer.

- Determine how you will do spiritual warfare, and with your focus on Jesus, step out in faith that demonic powers will be overcome.

DAY 26: PRAYER OF AGREEMENT

When I pray I am conscious of being aligned with God's Word and Spirit.

1   2   3   4   5   6   7   8   9   10

When I pray with others, I find a point of agreement.

1   2   3   4   5   6   7   8   9   10

- Evaluate yourself on things you presently pray for. Are you praying in agreement with God's Word and Spirit?

- The next time you pray for someone, find a point of agreement in faith before praying.

DAY 27: SERVING THOSE WE PRAY FOR

I look for ways to serve people I pray for.

1   2   3   4   5   6   7   8   9   10

I serve people I pray for—and pray for people I serve.

1   2   3   4   5   6   7   8   9   10

- Actively look for ways you can serve others—and pray for them while you serve.

- Begin praying for people you already serve in work or volunteer situations.

DAY 28: WRITING IT DOWN

I write down prophecies, answers to prayer, and impressions from the Lord.

1   2   3   4   5   6   7   8   9   10

I keep some kind of journal of my Christian growth experience.

1   2   3   4   5   6   7   8   9   10

- Create a folder or notebook or something in which to stash notes on prayers God has answered. Review them and be encouraged.

- Keep a prayer journal of thoughts, insights, and words from God you have had while praying.

DAY 29: RAISING VOICES TOGETHER

My prayer group experiences are awesome.

1   2   3   4   5   6   7   8   9   10

When I pray in a group, my participation is very active.

1   2   3   4   5   6   7   8   9   10

- Join a prayer group at your local church, your school, or your workplace.

- Pray together with people in your household. Start with praying once a week and increase from there.

DAY 30: MAXIMUM EXPOSURE

I maintain an open-minded yet discerning approach to things I'm not used to.

1   2   3   4   5   6   7   8   9   10

I learn as much as I can from people who have gone before me.

1   2   3   4   5   6   7   8   9   10

- Study and apply to yourself a Bible verse (or attend a Christian meeting or pray with someone) that has made you uncomfortable.
- Assess yourself on your attitude toward new or different things. Name one thing toward which you could be more open.

NOTES

First Word

1. Mother Teresa, quoted in Becky Benenate and Joseph Durepos, eds., *Mother Teresa: No Greater Love* (Novato, CA: New World Library, 1989), 4.

Day 1 Hunger for God

1. A. W. Tozer, *The Pursuit of God* (Harrisburg, PA: Christian Publications, n.d.), 17.

2. John of the Cross, *The Ascent of Mount Carmel*, in *The Collected Works of St. John of the Cross*, trans. Kieran Kavanaugh and Otilio Rodriguez (Washington DC: Institute of Carmelite Studies, 1979), 7.

Day 2 Intimacy with God

1. J. Paul Reno, *Daniel Nash: Prevailing Prince of Prayer* (Asheville, NC: Revival Literature, 1989), 3–7.

2. Teresa of Avila, *The Interior Castle*, in *The Collected Works of St. Teresa of Avila*, vol. 2, trans. Otilio Rodriguez and Kieran Kavanaugh (Washington DC: Institute of Carmelite Studies, 1980), 434.

3. Ibid., 283.

4. Dietrich Bonhoeffer, *The Cost of Discipleship* (New York: Macmillan, 1963), 99.

Day 3 Holy Passion

1. Richard Foster, *Celebration of Discipline: The Path to Spiritual Growth* (San Francisco: HarperSanFrancisco, 1998), 15.

2. J. B. Phillips, *Your God Is Too Small* (London: The Epworth Press, 1952), vii.

Day 4 Starting a Dead Engine

1. Though the prayer is attributed to St. Francis, the earliest known printed version of this was in French in 1912. See http://en.wikipedia.org/wiki/Prayer_of_Saint_Francis.

Day 5 Getting a Faith Lift

1. Basil Miller, *George Müller: Man of Faith and Miracles* (Minneapolis: Bethany House Publishers, 1941), 56.

2. Ibid., 55, emphasis in original.

3. George Müller, quoted in ibid., 53–54.

4. Kenneth Hagin, *Exceedingly Growing Faith* (Tulsa, OK: Faith Library Publications, 1983), 51–54.

Day 6 Cleaning House

1. Bernard of Clairvaux, "On the Steps of Humility and Pride," in *Bernard of Clairvaux: Selected Works*, trans. G. R. Evans (New York: Paulist Press, 1987), 115.

Day 7 Character Growth

1. *Shadowlands*, directed by Richard Attenbury (1993; HBO Home Video, 1999).

2. C. S. Lewis, *The Problem of Pain* (New York: Macmillan, 1962), 93.

Day 8 Praise Power

1. I first grasped this idea through the teaching of LaMar Boschman.

2. Quoted in Loren Wilkinson, "Saving Celtic Christianity," *Christianity Today*, April 24, 2000, 84.

3. Terry Law, *The Power of Praise and Worship* (Tulsa, OK: Victory House, 1985), 156, emphasis in original.

Day 9 Spirit Led

1. D. Elton Trueblood, *The People Called Quakers* (New York: Harper & Row, 1966), 86.

2. Ibid., 88, emphasis in original.

Day 10 Practicing God's Presence

1. Brother Lawrence, *The Practice of the Presence of God*, ed. Douglas V. Steere (Nashville: The Upper Room, 1950), 35.

2. Joseph de Beaufort, quoted in ibid., 21.

3. Brother Lawrence, *The Practice of the Presence of God*, ed. Donald Demaray (New York: Alba House, 1997), 9.

4. Brother Lawrence, *Practice*, ed. Douglas V. Steere, 7.

5. Mother Teresa, "Mother Teresa Quote," I Love India, May 6, 2008, http://www.iloveindia.com/indian-heroes/mother-teresa/quote.html.

6. Archibald Hart, "Renewing the Heart" (lecture, Nazarene District Pastors' Retreat, Los Angeles, October 3, 2000).

7. Frank Laubach, *Practicing His Presence*, ed. Gene Edwards (Goleta, CA: Christian Books, 1973), 15.

Day 11 A Time to Listen

1. Postmodernism tends to exhibit four major tendencies: (1) it rejects the idea that reason is the best way to discern truth and reality; (2) it views the individual as being defined, even determined, by a social situation, especially race, class, and gender; (3) it is thoroughly relativistic—since truth, like people, is socially constructed, there is no absolute truth; and (4) it insists that therefore people must be tolerant of the views and practices of all other people and not impose any moral standard.

2. O. Hallesby, *Prayer*, trans. C. J. Carlsen (London: Inter-Varsity Fellowship, 1961), 74–75.

3. R. A. Torrey, *How to Pray* (New Kensington, PA: Whitaker House, 1983), 44.

Day 12 Lifted Voice

1. Tony Campolo (lecture, Fuller Theological Seminary, Pasadena, CA, 1985).

Day 13 Specifically Speaking

1. Andrew Murray, *With Christ in the School of Prayer* (Grand Rapids: Zondervan, 1983), 47.

Day 14 Praying God's Word

1. Norman Williams, public testimony, Los Angeles, 1978.

2. Jeanne Guyon, *Experiencing the Depths of Jesus Christ*, trans. Gene Edwards (Auburn, ME: Christian Books, 1975), 8, emphasis in original.

Day 15 The Empty-Stomach Effect

1. Jerry Falwell, quoted in Christine J. Gardner, "Hungry for God: Why More and More Christians Are Fasting for Revival," *Christianity Today*, April 5, 1999, 34.

2. Peter Chrysologus, quoted in R. D. Chatham, *Fasting: A Biblical-Historical Study* (South Plainfield, NJ: Bridge Publishing, 1987), 82.

3. Don Colbert, *The Seven Pillars of Health* (Lake Mary, FL: Siloam, 2007), 177–78.

Day 17 Special Appointments

1. Allen Carden, *Puritan Christianity in America* (Grand Rapids: Baker, 1990), 131.

2. From her poem "By Night When Others Soundly Slept":

I sought him whom my Soul did Love,
With tears I sought him earnestly.
He bow'd his ear down from Above.
In vain I did not seek or cry.

My hungry Soul he fill'd with Good;
He in his Bottle put my tears,
My smarting wounds washt in his blood,
And banisht thence my Doubts and fears.

See http://www.annebradstreet.com/by_night_when_others_soundly_slept.html.

3. Richard Foster, *Prayer: Finding the Heart's True Home* (San Francisco: Harper Collins, 1992), 162.

4. Basil Miller, *John Wesley* (Minneapolis: Bethany House Publishers, 1943), 98.

Day 18 Lifted Hands and Feet

1. George Tortora and Nicholas Anagnostakos, *Principles of Anatomy and Physiology*, 5th ed. (New York: Harper and Row, 1987), 310.

Day 19 Guides or No Guides

1. Evagrius Ponticus, *The Praktikos & Chapters on Prayer*, trans. John Bamberger (Kalamazoo, MI: Cistercian Publications, 1981), 34.

2. Ibid., 20.

Day 20 Minimizing Distractions

1. See Matthew 16:23; Luke 22:31; John 13:2; Acts 5:3; and 2 Corinthians 11:3.

2. Ponticus, *Praktikos*, 29.

Day 21 Unanswered Prayer

1. Foster, *Prayer*, 20.

2. Two classics in the area of healing inner wounds are David Seamands, *Healing of Memories* (Wheaton, IL: Victor Books, 1985), and John and Paula Sandford, *The Transformation of the Inner Man* (South Plainfield, NJ: Bridge Publishing, 1982).

3. For a comprehensive, well-researched, commonsense, Christian volume on health, I recommend Don Colbert, *The Seven Pillars of Health*.

4. Tom White, *Breaking Strongholds* (Ann Arbor, MI: Servant Publications, 1993), 24.

Day 24 Persistent Boldness

1. Torrey, *How to Pray*, 50.
2. Basil Miller, *Praying Hyde* (Grand Rapids: Zondervan, 1943), 7.

Day 27 Serving Those We Pray For

1. Mother Teresa, *No Greater Love* (Novato, CA: New World Library, 1997), 40.
2. Ibid., 72.
3. Abbe Pierre, quoted in Philip Yancey, *Reaching for the Invisible God* (Grand Rapids: Zondervan, 2000), 239–40.
4. Brother Lawrence, *Practice*, ed. Donald Demaray, 35.

Day 29 Raising Voices Together

1. Norman Grubb, *Rees Howells: Intercessor* (Fort Washington, PA: Christian Literature Crusade, 1952), 234.
2. Ibid., 236.
3. Ibid., 241.
4. Bruce Wilkinson, interview by James Dobson, *Focus on the Family*, 1984.
5. Ibid.
6. Ibid.
7. Foster, *Prayer*, 176.
8. Ruth A. Tucker, *From Jerusalem to Irian Jaya* (Grand Rapids: Zondervan, 1983), 71.

Peter Lundell is a former missionary to Japan and now co-pastors the Walnut Blessing Church of the Nazarene in Walnut, California. He is the founder of the Walnut Valley Pastors' Prayer Network. He holds a master of divinity and doctor of missiology from Fuller Theological Seminary and is the author of several books. You can visit him at www.PeterLundell.com.

MEET PETER LUNDELL

• • •

VISIT WWW.PETERLUNDELL.COM

- Read the blog
- Sign-up to receive the newsletter
- Find free resources

GET IN THE CONVERSATION!

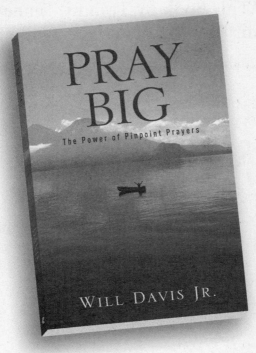

"I am alive today because of the kind of bold praying you'll find in *Pray Big*. This important book can change your expectations about prayer, challenging you to seek God much more intimately, to ask for audacious requests more boldly, and to see big answers to prayer that change lives for eternity."

—DON PIPER, bestselling author, *90 Minutes in Heaven*

Revell
a division of Baker Publishing Group
www.RevellBooks.com

Available Wherever Books Are Sold

"This book by Tommy Tenney confirms what I have felt all along."
—Stormie Omartian

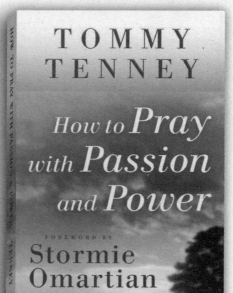

Prayer will change your life!

Revell
a division of Baker Publishing Group
www.RevellBooks.com

Available Wherever Books Are Sold

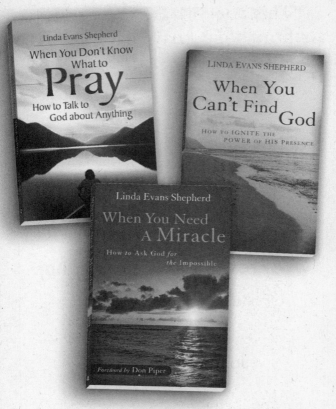

"Linda has used powerful prayer to overcome the worst of circumstances, and you can too. She does not share pat answers, she shares truth that will transform your life."

—LeAnn Thieman, coauthor, *Chicken Soup for the Christian Woman's Soul*

Revell
a division of Baker Publishing Group
www.RevellBooks.com

Available Wherever Books Are Sold
Also Available in Ebook Format

Be the First to Hear about Other New Books from Revell!

Sign up for announcements about new and upcoming titles at

www.revellbooks.com/signup

Follow us on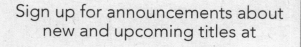
RevellBooks

Join us on facebook
Revell

Don't miss out on our great reads!

Revell
a division of Baker Publishing Group
www.RevellBooks.com